THE 50 *Fridays*

MARRIAGE CHALLENGE

One Question a Week
One Incredib...

"This practical and inspiring book will help husbands and wives reach their God-given potential. I highly recommend it!"

—GARY CHAPMAN, PhD, author of *The 5 Love Languages*

JEFF & LORA HELTON

Praise for
The 50 Fridays Marriage Challenge

"Most couples desire a loving, supportive marriage in which husband and wife are helping each other reach their potential for God. However, many couples do not have a plan for creating such a marriage. In *The 50 Fridays Marriage Challenge*, Jeff and Lora Helton provide a plan. I highly recommend it."

—Gary Chapman, PhD, author of *The 5 Love Languages*

"*The 50 Fridays Marriage Challenge* is a terrific adventure worth your time and focus! The Heltons have masterfully woven together fifty questions that will result in you growing closer to God and one another. My only complaint is that it's two Fridays short of an entire year!!!"

—Dr. Dennis Rainey, host of *FamilyLife Today*

"I've been married to my beautiful wife, Sharon, for thirty years. We've laughed, worked, played, talked, and argued our way through some pretty incredible times, and trust me, it wasn't always easy! Marriage is hard work, but it's the best, most rewarding work I've ever done—and it's something you need to work at, too. In *The 50 Fridays Marriage Challenge*, Jeff and Lora will walk you and your spouse through a fantastic yearlong discussion that will totally change your marriage!"

—Dave Ramsey, *New York Times* bestselling author
and nationally syndicated radio show host

"Most men avoid 'talk about the relationship' conversations, fearing the inevitable feelings of inadequacy and unmet expectations. But Jeff and Lora Helton have developed fifty conversation starters that will have you relishing your time together. You'll not only strengthen your marriage, you'll have fun in the process!"

—Marshall Shelley, vice president, *Christianity Today*

"I have had the privilege of knowing Jeff and Lora while they were on staff at our home church in Brentwood, TN. When my husband, Stu, and I were approaching the twenty-year mark of marriage, we felt the need to recalibrate and take some time to get to know each other again. With the constant pull of his work, our kids, and my years of traveling, we had come to a place of 'coasting.' We didn't want to be one of those couples whose kids went off to college and they sat staring at one another not knowing who each other were anymore. Many of the suggestions in this book are questions that Jeff had us ask each other. Whether married one year, twenty years, or fifty years, we could all use a tune-up. Marriage is worth it."

—Denise Jones, Point of Grace, popular Christian singing group

"This book is a true gift to all of us who are seeking stronger marriages. Jeff and Lora have provided us with an incredible guide to help challenge and revitalize our relationships. My wife and I are so thankful for *The 50 Fridays Marriage Challenge*."

—Pete Wilson, senior pastor, Cross Point Church, Nashville, TN, and author of *Plan B*

"Sometimes you recommend a book based just on its content. Other times you might recommend a book because of your relationship to the author. And occasionally you recommend a book based on both. I have the privilege of knowing and serving with Jeff and Lora Helton. The principles and concepts of this book are far more than content; they are the realities of married life being lived out, modeled, and shared by these two wonderful friends. *The 50 Fridays Marriage Challenge* will do just that; it will challenge you to rethink, refocus, and recommit to your marriage. This is not just another book on marriage, this is a book of encouragement written by two very authentic people who are committed to helping others build better marriages."

—Rick White, senior pastor, the People's Church, Franklin, TN

"*The 50 Fridays Marriage Challenge* is a fun way to use conversation starters for husbands and wives. They open the door for meaningful discussions in a nonthreatening way. Praying for and with one another is a way for your marriage to thrive and survive. Learning more about each other makes for a solid, exciting relationship. Lora and Jeff cover real issues with tried-and-true ways to have a strong, healthy marriage. We have enjoyed going through the book ourselves and look forward to sharing it with those we mentor."

—Marsha and Jack Countryman, bestselling author
and creator of God's Promises line

"I remember the year that Jeff and Lora wrote these questions—one Friday after another, after another, after another. And I remember the change that God wrought in them—Jeff in particular—as I saw the very questions he was asking reshape and refine his own heart. It will do the same for every couple who refuses the 'default mode' and chooses to take the challenge."

—Lloyd Shadrach, teaching pastor,
Fellowship Bible Church, Brentwood, TN

"*The 50 Fridays Marriage Challenge* is a fun and practical approach to strengthening marriages. Each challenge is thought-provoking, intentional, and encourages an opportunity for true intimacy. We've personally encountered Jeff and Lora's love and counsel in our own lives. What a treasure it is to now have access to their wealth of wisdom through this book. If you're willing to take the challenge, you will definitely be inspired to pursue the marriage God intended for you to have."

—Joe Katina, The Katinas

THE

50

Fridays

MARRIAGE CHALLENGE

One Question a Week. One Incredible Marriage.

JEFF AND LORA HELTON

HOWARD BOOKS
A DIVISION OF SIMON & SCHUSTER, INC.
New York • Nashville • London • Toronto • Sydney • New Delhi

Howard Books
A Division of Simon & Schuster, Inc.
1230 Avenue of the Americas
New York, NY 10020

First Howard Books trade paperback edition September 2013

HOWARD and colophon are trademarks of Simon & Schuster, Inc.

For information about special discounts for bulk purchases,
please contact Simon & Schuster Special Sales at
1-866-506-1949 or business@simonandschuster.com.

The Simon & Schuster Speakers Bureau can bring authors to your live event.
For more information or to book an event contact the Simon & Schuster Speakers Bureau
at 1-866-248-3049 or visit our website at www.simonspeakers.com.

Designed by Ruth Lee-Mui

Manufactured in the United States of America

1   3   5   7   9   10   8   6   4   2

Library of Congress Cataloging-in-Publication Data
Helton, Jeff.
The 50 Fridays marriage challenge : one question a week.
one incredible marriage. / Jeff and Lora Helton.
    pages   cm
1. Marriage—Religious aspects—Christianity. 2. Marriage.
I. Helton, Lora. II. Title. III. Title: Fifty Fridays marriage challenge.
BV835.H454   2013
248.8'44—dc23   2013001169

ISBN 978-1-4767-0500-2
ISBN 978-1-4767-0501-9 (ebook)

To our parents, who taught us that fifty years of marriage happens one Friday at a time.

To Lora's parents, Lionel and Marion: fifty-three years and going strong as trendsetters in multicultural marriage. Your faith, commitment, and care for others are a model worthy of imitation.

To Jeff's dad, Ray, who experienced more than fifty years of marriages by loving and burying two wives (Mildred and Nancy). Your eternal perspective and confidence in God's goodness and plan inspire us daily.

Contents

Introduction   1

THE 50 CHALLENGES

Contents

BONUS SECTION

INTRODUCTION

What Will Your Marriage Be Like on Your Fiftieth Anniversary?

In 2009, we traveled to Bismarck, North Dakota, to celebrate Lora's parents' fiftieth wedding anniversary. My in-laws have spent their entire marriage in vocational ministry—serving as missionaries in Indonesia and Malaysia and traveling around the globe. Overall, they have aged really well and have remained in good health. As we watched the slide show of their fifty years together, I was struck with the reality of what fifty years do to a person's hair color, muscle tone, skin elasticity, and waistline.

At the time, Lora and I had been married for twenty-two years, and I found my mind wandering and wondering about what our fiftieth anniversary would be like. More accurately, I started thinking about what we would *look* like. I did the math. I'll be seventy-seven. Lora will be . . . well . . . less than that.

I glanced at my in-laws and thought, *What will we look like? Will there be more wrinkles? A few more pounds? What color hair? Will I even have hair?*

If we ever do stop and think about what our marriage will be like at fifty years, we all too often think only about the external—the physical. But the truth is, there's a far more important question to ponder: Should the Lord allow us to make it to fifty years of marriage, what will we *be* like at our fiftieth anniversary?

In other words . . . will we finish strong?

- Will we be thriving? Or will we be surviving?
- Will we be enjoying an intimate and connected marriage? Or will we be two strangers living in the same home?
- Will we intentionally be wise in how we spend our days? Or will we foolishly let the months and years pass by?

Psalm 90:12 says, "Teach us to number our days aright, that we may gain a heart of wisdom." Psalm 90 is the oldest psalm and was written by Moses toward the end of the time of Israel's wandering in the wilderness. Those days were filled with challenges, grumbling, frustrations, and difficulties. Throughout the psalm, Moses reminds the Israelites of how quickly this life passes by: "A thousand years in your sight are like a day that has just gone by" (verse 4). He also reminds them that we have only a finite number of days: "Our days may come to seventy years, or eighty, if our strength endures; yet the best of them are but trouble and sorrow, for they quickly pass, and we fly away" (verse 10).

Every time I read those words from Psalm 90, I'm reminded of how quickly time goes by. We recently celebrated twenty-five years of marriage, and it feels like our wedding day was only yesterday. It seems like our children were just born, and yet two of them are in college and our younger two sons are in high school. The past twenty-five years have flown! And for that matter, *fifty* years fly by as well—especially in our marriages.

When we first start out on our marriage adventure, it seems that we have forever ahead of us. And then, life happens. Babies come along. Career paths change. School starts. Finances get tight. And before you know it, life is going faster than you realize.

In the midst of all of this, many couples become passive in their approach to their marriage and wake up one day wondering what went wrong. They operate their marriages in what we call *default mode*: things happen without planning or intentionality or effort. Instead of the default mode, we need a proactive approach for our marriages to grow. The call that we're sending out is this: Get out of the default mode in your marriage. Live at a higher level! There has to be a plan. The old adage is right: *Fail to plan, plan to fail.*

When marriages are not actively nurtured, they tend to go into the default mode. Usually this means that our sinful nature will be more active than our desire to please God. The default mode is where selfishness grows and flourishes. Here criticism of your spouse is accepted and even encouraged by friends. It is where fantasy tends to have a greater pull than reality and where hope for a better marriage dies.

In the default mode, we get stuck in ruts. Perhaps you have had the exact same fights with your spouse over and over again, without acceptable resolution. Most couples do, because most couples live their marriages on automatic. When you get right down to it, the main problem is often that couples do not prioritize the time necessary to keep a marriage growing and alive.

A proactive approach to marriage says that this relationship is so important to you that you are going to actively ensure its success and health with preventive medicine and a focus on growth rather than crisis management. Therefore, you are willing to put in the time and intentionality required to ensure your success.

We find it interesting that one of the struggles we have with couples whom we are counseling is getting them to commit to time each week with each other. Many insist that the time isn't there. If you're one of these people, we would like you to consider how much time you spend:

- Watching television
- Working extra hours
- Going to movies
- Working on a committee
- Reading
- Talking to friends
- Watching or participating in sports
- Shopping for fun
- Doing your favorite hobby
- Playing on the computer
- Doing volunteer work
- Attending or running church activities

We contend that if you have time to do any or many of these activities, you have time to spend on your marriage. Are any of these more important than your marriage?

"Wait a second!" you might say. "Church activities are on that list! Isn't that a good thing on which to spend time?" Of course, but we've met many good Christians who help out at church yet treat their spouses in a very dishonoring way, not giving the spouse the time she or he deserves. We greatly believe in serving Christ by volunteering at church but believe that the church would grow stronger and more authentic if members would prioritize having a godly marriage even over helping at the church. Our position is that if you build a healthier marriage, you will have more energy and actually be more effective in helping at your church.

The state of many marriages is busyness. We often see it in the couples we counsel. It's not that they don't love each other. It's not that their problems are so great that they can't deal with them. Often, their lack of intentionality to grow and guard their marriage has them in a place where they don't feel connected anymore. They've stopped being vulnerable and intentional. Intimacy suffers. Weeks or even months tend to pass without having an honest dialogue about how their marriage is really doing. But that's not how things started.

Nearly every couple who stood in front of a church on their wedding day exchanged vows and longed for an intimate, authentic, and growing marriage. No one stands there with their fingers crossed during the "to have and to hold" part of the vows. We were excited and confident and hopeful for what the future had in store. That's how Lora and I started our marriage. But around year six, we found ourselves busy with children and, in many ways, going through the motions of our marriage. And then four great couples reached out to us, and we began to connect with them weekly, spending most of our time together intentionally growing our marriage through authentic and vulnerable communication. Through those nights, we developed a plan that led us to deeper intentionality in tending to our marriage.

Every marriage can benefit from an intentional plan. What if there was a tool that would help you have a weekly intentional conversation about your marriage—a tool that would help you grow in spiritual, emotional, and physical intimacy?

That's where *The 50 Fridays Marriage Challenge* comes in! The challenge is simple and fun. Each week as a couple, you will spend a few minutes answering one question that has been designed to help you have open and honest conversation as you connect with and enjoy each other. Some weeks you will laugh as you travel down memory lane together. Some weeks you will be challenged as you evaluate different aspects of your marriage. And other weeks you will dream and plan for what the future can become. Our hope is that *The 50 Fridays Marriage Challenge* will give a troubled couple new hope, a happy couple a tool for ongoing closeness, and a newly married couple a unique way to know each other more deeply.

Intentionally growing intimacy in your marriage is such a valuable investment. The return on this investment brings a benefit far beyond your marriage. All of us are leaving a legacy through our marriages to our children and to our friends. We can choose the kind of legacy we leave; it may be a legacy that is marked by a lack of intentionality or even apathy. Or we can leave a legacy marked by an intentional way of connecting and enjoying the years ahead so they don't just pass us by.

Let's thrive, and not just survive, on the way to our golden anniversaries. After all, getting to fifty years starts with fifty Fridays!

1

A FRESH START

CHALLENGE 1

How will we use the 50 Fridays Marriage
Challenge each week?

Teach us to number our days aright, that we may gain
a heart of wisdom.

—*Psalm 90:12*

Life is busy. Among our jobs, hobbies, work, and shuttling
kids—it's easy to stay so busy that we miss intentionally caring
for and growing our marriages. Date night can become less
frequent. Tender moments slip away. Heartfelt conversations
vanish. And then we begin to wonder what's going on with
our intimacy.

If we're going to enjoy a healthy, God-honoring, intimate
marriage, we must intentionally invest in each other. By saying

"yes" to the 50 Fridays Marriage Challenge, you are declaring your desire to grow your marriage in spiritual, emotional, and physical intimacy. Accepting this challenge means that you're going to commit to a weekly intentional time to proactively engage with and talk about your marriage.

Today's question should lead you to think through your expectations and some of the logistics for the 50 Fridays Marriage Challenge. Take some time together to discuss how you will use each week's question. For example:

- When will you discuss the question? *(Bedtime might not be a good idea!)*
- Where will you discuss the question? *(Let me recommend face-to-face, not over the phone or by e-mail.)*
- Who will be responsible for initiating that time? *(Husbands, this is a great opportunity for us!)*
- How will you decide who answers the question first? *(Rock, paper, scissors?)*
- Will you commit to spend some time praying with each other at the end of the discussion?
- What will you do when one of the questions creates some tension?
- Would this be a good time to start a journal together?

Don't let any of these questions create pressure. There's not a right or a wrong way to do this. What works for your marriage is what matters. Remember, the purpose of the challenge is to encourage communication together. Sometimes it's hard work. But it's always worth it. So develop an intentional plan for how you'll use the 50 Fridays Marriage Challenge and then jump in!

Communicating is often a burdensome task, but it is a task that must be accomplished for a marriage to be complete. When communication falters, the marriage is in trouble. When it fails, the marriage is virtually doomed.

—R. C. Sproul, *The Intimate Marriage*

HERE I AM

CHALLENGE 2
How do you define intimacy?

For this reason a man will leave his father and mother and be united to his wife, and they will become one flesh. The man and his wife were both naked, and they felt no shame.

—Genesis 2:24–25

The word *intimacy* is one of those words that can have different meanings to different people. Some people think of deep conversations filled with emotional language as a perfect picture of intimacy. Others imagine walks on the beach as the sun is going down. For some the word *intimacy* is a synonym for sex (these people are generally called husbands).

A dictionary definition of *intimacy* reads: "a close, familiar, and usually affectionate or loving relationship with another person." But intimacy means so much more than that. The best way to define intimacy is to break the word down phonetically and let it define itself. Intimacy really is "in-to-me-see." Real intimacy is about transparency, vulnerability, and authenticity. It's allowing our spouse to see inside of us and to understand what's really going on.

We often mistake intensity for intimacy. For years, when our marriage was "in a funk," we would go on a bigger and better date night—or maybe slip away for a weekend to renew the spark. We were looking for a more intense encounter. Big date nights and romantic getaways are great for a marriage, but they don't ensure intimacy. Intimacy requires an intentional time to know and be known by speaking of the deepest parts of our souls.

Toward the end of Genesis 2, we see the first picture of intimacy between a man and a woman. God has created all of heaven and earth and then in his final act of creation makes a woman for Adam. In my imagination, I picture this perfect wedding day with Adam anticipating his wife and God the Father giving her away to him. In verse 25 of Genesis 2, the Bible says that they "were both naked, and they felt no shame." The literal and physical meaning of the word *naked* certainly needs to be acknowledged in this passage. But more than that, Adam and Eve experienced a "one flesh" unity: they were completely naked—physically, emotionally, intimately—and felt no shame.

When we allow our spouse to fully see and know us, that's when intimacy grows. Shame is the obvious barrier to being known by our spouse. Shame is that voice that says, "I can't tell her that" or "If he really saw this part of me . . ." Shame is defeated through unconditional love and acceptance. Ultimately, this is the gift of grace that comes from God, but often His greatest dispenser of that grace is our spouse. In our marriages, we must learn to accept each other "warts and all," as my grandmother often said. When our marriages our marked by that type of acceptance and grace-giving, it creates an environment where we can live naked and unashamed. And that's the environment when intimacy flourishes.

Try this exercise sometime this week: individually make a list of some of the barriers that keep you from sharing your thoughts, feelings, or desires with each other. Then talk through your lists together and look for ways to offer grace and understanding to each other.

For a marriage relationship to flourish there must be intimacy. It takes an enormous amount of courage to say to your spouse, "This is me. I'm not proud of it— in fact, I'm a little embarrassed by it—but this is who I am."

—Bill Hybels, *Who You Are When No One's Looking*

DELIGHTFULLY SEEN
AND KNOWN

CHALLENGE 3

What physical characteristic of your spouse
do you most enjoy?

For you created my inmost being; you knit me together in my mother's womb. I praise you because I
am fearfully and wonderfully made; your works are
wonderful, I know that full well. My frame was not
hidden from you when I was made in the secret place.
When I was woven together in the depths of the earth.

—*Psalm 139:13–15*

My dad loved my mom's hands.

I can remember as a teenage boy often hearing my dad
say to my mother how much he liked her hands. He described

15

them as "petite, beautiful, and perfect." I would think, "They're just hands. What's the big deal? One day, I'll find something better than hands to like about my wife!"

Years later, after my mom died, I walked into the kitchen one day where Dad was washing dishes at the sink. As I got closer to him I saw tears running down his cheeks, and I asked him what was going on. I'll never forget his reply, "Every time that I see soap bubbles in a sink, I can see your mom's hands washing so many dishes through the years. I miss her. I miss her hands that served and loved us so well."

It's good and it is right for us to enjoy the physical attributes of our spouse. Even a quick reading through the Song of Solomon allows us to see how a young couple delighted in each other's bodies (wives read Song of Solomon 5:10–16 and husbands read Song of Solomon 7:1–9). In these two passages we find very poetic, yet sensual, descriptions of how these young lovers dream about and see each other's body. Physical attributes can arouse desire. And that's good and right.

And yet the essence of lasting love is not just in the physical—it's a deeper and more intimate connection that sees and knows each other deeply . . . intimately . . . passionately . . . tenderly. An intimate marriage celebrates and enjoys the inside of our spouse even more than the outside. Sometimes we forget that in our image-oriented culture.

In the course of my parents' marriage, my dad came to understand that the physical beauty of my mom's hands actually pointed to something of even greater significance—the character of his wife. For Dad, Mom's hands represented her gentle touch, her acts of service, and her compassionate heart for him and for our family.

Enjoy this week's question. It gives you an opportunity to delight in and compliment different physical characteristics of your spouse. As you share your answers with each other, remember that time has a way of changing, reshaping, and even wrinkling the physical. But when we see the physical as an expression of the internal, our appreciation of beauty and strength in our spouse grows through the years.

To view our spouse from the lens of glory is to be overwhelmed by the privilege of being face-to-face with a creature who mirrors God.

—Dan Allender and Tremper Longman III, *Intimate Allies*

4

LET'S ENJOY LIFE

CHALLENGE 4

What hobbies or activities do you enjoy in your marriage?
What other things would you like to do together?

A cheerful heart is good medicine, but a crushed spirit
dries up the bones.

—*Proverbs 17:22*

One Saturday afternoon, Lora spoke the most incredible words
to me.

Let me set the scene: It was a rainy day in middle Ten-
nessee, sometime around 3:00 on a Saturday afternoon in
October. The television had been on since 9:00 a.m.—after
all, that's when *College GameDay* starts! In my humble opinion, fall Saturdays were created for the purpose of watching
college football.

Enter Lora. She had been out for most of the morning and came home to find me in pretty much the same place I had been when she left—in front of the TV watching football flanked by two of our sons. It was at that moment that she spoke these amazing words: "I like having football games on the television. It's fun to see you and the boys watching the game."

WOW! What a moment. Never such intimacy and connection between a man and a woman! I mean, she was speaking my love language in a profound way. I thought, *I think we've finally found a hobby that we both enjoy! I'll watch college football with our sons, and Lora can watch us watching it!*

That's not exactly how hobbies work. However, developing shared hobbies *together* can be an asset for any marriage. When we discover something we enjoy together, that activity can provide a unique place for connection, fun, and memory building. When you think of a hobby, it doesn't have to require a great amount of money. It could be anything: walking, biking, hiking, cooking, gardening, dancing, golf, tennis, bowling, traveling, eating out, playing games, or even watching football together. The list is limitless. The key is to find something you both enjoy and then take the time to actually do it. Marriage certainly has a lot of moments that are filled with hard work. That's one of the reasons we need to be intentional about hobbies that bring fun and relaxation into our marriage. Here's an easy way to brainstorm a hobby list this week. If your refrigerator is like ours, you probably have several magnets on it holding important pictures and lists! Add a blank sheet of paper with the word "hobbies" written at the top, and throughout the week add things you'd enjoy doing with your spouse. Sometime next week, pull the list down and circle a couple of things for you to try together.

The Book of Ecclesiastes is filled with wisdom about the folly and brevity of this life. Time and again, Solomon says that this life is fleeting and that so much of what we do is vain and unimportant. And yet in the middle of chapter 9, Solomon encourages us to enjoy life with the one you love. As you're thinking about ways to enjoy time with each other this week, read Solomon's words in Ecclesiastes 9:7–9 in a few different translations. His encouragement, in the midst of life, is to make time to really enjoy each other and the pleasures of this life. That's good medicine for our marriages!

> People are often enamored with my Super Bowl ring. But it's my wedding ring that I'm most proud of. And having a good marriage takes even more work than winning a Super Bowl.
>
> —Trent Dilfer, former NFL quarterback, smartmarriages.com

FOR BETTER, FOR WORSE

CHALLENGE 5

What are three strengths of your marriage?
What one area would you like to see growth in?

Get wisdom, get understanding; do not forsake my
words or swerve from them. Do not forsake wisdom
and she will protect you; love her, and she will watch
over you.

—*Proverbs 4:5–6*

In Psalm 90:12, the Bible invites us to "number our days
aright, that we may gain a heart of wisdom." The idea of
"numbering our days" has nothing to do with counting or
with math. Rather, it means to evaluate or to consider. When
was the last time that, as a couple, you *intentionally* evaluated
the state of your marriage? I don't mean, when did you last

get into a fight? Or when was the last time one of you complained about something you don't like? Rather, do you have a regular time of proactively and intentionally checking in on how your marriage is doing?

An intentional evaluation of our marriages provides an opportunity for a couple of things to happen. First, there's a chance to celebrate together. Every marriage has some "sweet spots"—those places where life together is good and relatively easy. Strong places in our marriages need to be remembered and celebrated. New opportunities for growth in your marriage are often connected to your strengths. In other words, build on the natural strengths that you already have in your marriage.

Second, an intentional evaluation provides a place to honestly discuss areas where growth is needed. Every marriage also has some "hot spots"—those places where conflict most frequently occurs or where a marriage gets stuck. Having open and candid dialogue about places where growth and change are desired needs to happen intentionally and not just in the midst of a conflict. Change in our marriage can only begin when we talk about our dissatisfaction and desires.

Psalm 90:12 ends by telling us that we need to number our days to "gain a heart of wisdom." As you evaluate your marriage honestly and openly, know that you're growing in wisdom. So share your personal perspective—you don't have to agree (matter of fact, you probably won't!). Listen and consider the area of growth that your spouse desires to see in your relationship. Don't try to solve it all this week—you can't. But you can start on a journey of celebrating your "sweet spots" and brainstorming some steps to take in your "hot spots" as you continue to intentionally connect and grow intimacy in your marriage.

> Lord, when we are wrong, make us willing to change,
> and when we are right, make us easy to live with.
> —Peter Marshall, former US Senate chaplain

6

CONNECTING SPIRITUALLY

CHALLENGE 6

What is one tangible way that you can improve
your spiritual intimacy together?

For where two or three come together in my name,
there am I with them.

—*Jesus in Matthew 18:20*

Lora and I spent a wonderful evening with some good friends who had recently sent their youngest child to college. They were entering into a new season of their marriage: empty-nesters. We were curious to hear how their lives and their marriage had changed.

One of the first things they mentioned was how much they enjoy going to the Saturday-night church service their church offers. Since they have made this transition, Sundays have become a real day of rest—even Sabbath-like. On Sunday mornings, they spend time reading the Bible together and sharing insights. They have an extended prayer time. They spend time in silence.

As they shared this newfound routine with us, I found myself jealous at this opportunity afforded them. Like many of you, Lora and I certainly aren't in the season of life to leisurely spend a morning together weekly. Then I realized I wasn't really envious of the free time that our friends have. Rather, their comments stirred a longing in me for greater intentionality with Lora in our spiritual life together.

It's easy to get in a rut in any area of our marriages—especially in how we connect spiritually. How are you doing in that area? Are you proactively and intentionally growing your spiritual intimacy? What does your prayer life *together* look like? Family Life Ministries recently surveyed thousands of couples from their Weekend to Remember marriage getaways and discovered that less than 8 percent of all couples pray together on a regular basis!

For us, we often fall into the routine of praying *for* each other but rarely praying *with* each other. But something special happens when a couple prays together. To pray together requires a level of intimacy, vulnerability, and trust that impacts every area of our marriages.

If this is an area where your marriage can grow, the good news is that you can start today. Make it short and simple. You can do it right now: Each of you can share a specific prayer request and then take thirty seconds and pray together. It really is that simple, and it can be the beginning of tremendous growth in your spiritual life together.

Our marriages always benefit from intentional spiritual intimacy together.

A magnificent marriage begins not with knowing one another but with knowing God.

—Gary Thomas, *Sacred Marriage*

7

COME CLOSER!

CHALLENGE 7

Evaluate your physical intimacy. Where are you satisfied?
What would you like to see changed?

His left arm is under my head, and His right arm embraces me.

—*Song of Solomon 2:6*

When you saw this week's question, what came to your mind? For many men, the first thought was, *Finally! A question about sex!* But today's question is broader than just the topic of sex. The question today invites each couple to talk about physical intimacy (don't worry, men; there will be some specific questions about sexual intimacy soon).

Physical intimacy certainly includes sexual intimacy, but it includes many others acts of touch—hand holding, hugs, sitting close to each other on the couch, foot rubs, massages, tender kisses, cuddling, and so much more. It's the things that most of us did naturally when we were dating. And yet over time, it's easy to stop doing those things, and then we miss out on some special and tender moments together. Often it's these simple things that communicate not only our love for our spouse but also how much we like and enjoy being with our spouse.

Over the past decade or so, a lot of research has been conducted on the positive power of touch to increase relational connection. It really makes sense when you consider that touch is actually the first language we learn. Researchers have discovered that high-touch people are more connected, less stressed, more trusting, and maybe better basketball players! One study looked at the number of touches (high fives, chest bumps, hugs, etc.) between teammates on NBA basketball teams during the 2009 season. To the surprise of researchers, the good teams seem to be touchier than bad teams!

The power of touch is a great way to grow intimacy in our marriages. There's a great benefit in evaluating your physical intimacy. There's even a greater benefit in enjoying it together. One practical way to start this conversation may be to agree upon several areas that fall under the broader category of physical intimacy, such as holding hands, hugs, massages, kissing, cuddling, etc. Once you've established the areas that you would like to see as part of your marriage, talk through each category and create a vision of what you'd like to see your physical intimacy be like. Be prepared for there to be some dissatisfaction for each of you in one or more of the areas. That's not a problem; rather, it identifies places to address and grow. Change often starts with a picture of the future that you would like to enjoy together.

> Too often we underestimate the power of a touch, a smile, a kind word, a listening ear, an honest compliment, or the smallest act of caring, all of which have the potential to turn a life around.
>
> —Leo Buscaglia, *Born for Love*

START DREAMING

CHALLENGE 8

What is your "wildest dream" vacation? (Don't worry about the cost or any logistics . . . remember, it's a dream vacation!)

God can do anything, you know—far more than you could ever imagine or guess or request in your wildest dreams! He does it not by pushing us around but by working within us, His Spirit deeply and gently within us.

—Ephesians 3:20–21, The Message

Several years ago, one of our children had a school project that required planning a vacation out of the country, and he chose Madrid, Spain, as his destination. For the project, he had to create a PowerPoint presentation that included how he would get there, where he would stay, the restaurants he would eat in, and the attractions he would visit. As I watched him practice his presentation on the night before he turned it in, I found myself wanting to go to Spain! Later that night I started looking at other places on the Internet that I would like to visit. With the help of Google Earth, I visited the Eiffel Tower, Buckingham Palace, and the Opera House in Sydney, Australia. I had a blast.

The reality is that most of the time I'm pretty practical about where I'd like to go or what I'd like to do. I rarely take the time to dream big. Not just about vacation locations, but also about a lot of things in life. It's easy to become overly practical and responsible. But there's a place for dreaming—especially in our marriages. Sometimes the dreaming can be just for fun (like today's question). Sometimes the dreaming can help us prepare for the future (financial savings, house changes, serving opportunities, etc.). Sometimes the dreaming allows us to envision what our marriages can become and where we can grow together.

As we dream, we arouse hope. When hope is awakened, it provides the opportunity for us to trust—not merely in our dreams—but to trust that God's plan for our lives and marriages is better than anything we can ask, think, or even dream. In other words, our dreaming allows our hearts to be open to trust that God's plan is even better than our plans and dreams! In Eugene Peterson's paraphrase of the Book of Ephesians, he writes: "God can do anything, you know—far more than you could ever imagine or guess or request in your wildest dreams!

He does it not by pushing us around but by working within us, his Spirit deeply and gently within us" (*Ephesians 3:20–21, The Message*).

So as you dream together this week, be reminded that God is always at work to see His good purposes accomplished. Dream and allow hope to rise. As that happens, watch as God accomplishes His good and perfect plan in your life—no matter where your vacation takes you this year!

I would rather live in a world where my life is surrounded by mystery than live in a world so small that my mind could comprehend it.

—Harry Emerson Fosdick, *The Meaning of
Prayer and the Secret of Victorious Living*

THUMBS-UP AND A WINK

CHALLENGE 9
How are you giving love in your marriage?
How do you like to receive love?

Love is patient, love is kind. It does not envy, it does not boast, it is not proud. It is not rude, it is not self-seeking, it is not easily angered, it keeps no record of wrongs. Love does not delight in evil but rejoices with the truth. It always protects, always trusts, always hopes, always perseveres.

—1 Corinthians 13:4–7

Trivia question: Who was "the Wizard of Westwood"?

Answer: John Wooden. John Wooden was the legendary basketball coach at UCLA for twenty-seven years. Wooden's wizard-like wisdom on the basketball court earned him the nickname "the Wizard of Westwood." He won ten NCAA National Championships within a twelve-year stretch, with seven championships coming in a row. Wooden died at ninety-nine years old but always loved the springtime—March Madness!

But John Wooden was more than a wizard of a basketball coach. He was a wizard at loving his wife, Nell. John and Nell were married for nearly fifty-three years until she passed away in 1985. Coach Wooden described Nellie as the only girl he ever kissed and said his last love was his first love. In his book *They Call Me Coach*, John wrote, "Her love, faith, and loyalty through all our years together are primarily responsible for what I am."

Since her death, Coach Wooden wrote a love letter to her on the twenty-first of every month to mark her passing. He spoke of her with such tenderness, love, and passion. Wooden wrote, "Just before each game [in high school] . . . when we made eye contact she'd give me a little thumbs-up, and I'd wink or nod back at her. That carried right through to the last game I ever coached. . . . She is the greatest thing that ever happened to me."

Pretty good stuff for a basketball coach, huh?

One of my favorite Wooden quotes is our marriage quote today. I think Wooden does a wonderful job connecting how we give love to each other. As you consider the Wizard's life and some of his other quotes in today's challenge, what are some practical ways you can give to your spouse and better love him or her in your marriage?

Love means many things. It means giving. It means sharing. It means forgiving. It means understanding. It means being patient. It means learning. And you must always consider the other side, the other person. You can give without loving, but you cannot love without giving.

—Coach John Wooden,
Wooden: A Legacy in Words and Images

10

LOL

CHALLENGE 10

What are some things that make you laugh out loud?

A happy heart makes the face cheerful.

—*Proverbs 15:13a*

When I was a young boy, my dad and I would listen to his favorite comedians on LPs for hours. Red Skelton, Flip Wilson, and Bill Cosby were always at the top of the list. In my late teens, we would watch the TV comedy *Sanford and Son* and identify with how the father-son combination reminded us of interactions we were having as I was beginning to navigate early adulthood. Although several decades have passed, I'm amazed at how often we can remember a line from one of those shared memories and still burst into uncontrollable laughter.

Laughter really is good medicine. Much research over the past few decades has shown that people with a sense of humor have fewer health problems and sickness than those who are humor-impaired. A University of Maryland study concluded that there is a strong connection between laughter and cardiovascular health. In other words, laughter is good for our hearts! It's really nothing new. Solomon taught this principle many years ago in our proverb today. We have all benefited from laughter, even in the strangest of times. Lora and I have had many conflicts interrupted by something that one of our children have said or done that completely defuses the tension and allows us to laugh. Our son Jacob is famous for one-line zingers that can completely change the attitude or tone of a conversation on which he's been eavesdropping. In that brief moment of levity, we recalibrate and are often able to engage the topic differently because of the power of laughing together.

There is, however, a word of caution to consider in this: Laughing together is very different from laughing at each other. Laughter can be used as a defense mechanism or as sarcasm that can cut our spouses. Using laughter or humor to cover over pain or conflict is never a good way to connect.

But when we laugh together in our marriages, humor can bring a lot of value: it can help us connect, it can help us cope, it helps us love better, it can create memories, and it can be a bridge to forgiveness. Learning to laugh together is a great practice to develop as you grow intimacy in your marriage.

Be on the lookout for things that make you laugh: movies, sitcoms, telling stories or jokes, certain friendships. Life is certainly serious and, at times, difficult. But there is "a time to laugh," and when we do, our marriages are richer and our hearts are healthier for it.

Laughter, on a daily basis, is like taking a vitamin for your marriage.

—Drs. Les and Leslie Parrott, *The Love List*

11

REMEMBER WHEN?

CHALLENGE 11

*What are some favorite memories from
your wedding day and honeymoon?*

May your fountain be blessed, and may you rejoice in
the wife of your youth.

—*Proverbs 5:18*

You may remember the Old Testament story of God parting
the Red Sea for Moses and the Israelites for them to escape
from the Egyptians. Later in Israel's history, God did something similar—He miraculously held back a river during flood
season in Joshua 3 so the Israelites could safely cross the Jordan
River on their way to the Promised Land.

In chapter 4, after they have successfully crossed the river,
God commanded them to build a memorial out of stones as

a sign for future generations to see His faithfulness and goodness. God knew there would be tough days in their future when they would need to remember His past acts of faithfulness and goodness. There's something really important about *remembering* in our faith development.

The same is true in our marriages. We need to take time to remember.

Here's an exercise for you to do together: Grab your Bible and read Joshua 3:1–4:8. Pay special attention to what's going on in the story and to how the people of Israel respond in order to remember God's goodness and faithfulness to them. Then "gather some stones and build your own memorial" today as you remember. There are a lot of ways to gather memory stones: Tell stories to your children or friends. Pull out the wedding photo album. Call someone from your wedding party whom you haven't talked to in a while. Watch your wedding video. Recount stories from your honeymoon. We were married in Chicago and flew out to Southern California for our honeymoon. On our first morning in Palm Springs, we learned one of our big differences: I like to sleep in and Lora loves to wake up early and be outside! Because of the time change, we were sitting outside in a hot tub together at 5:45 a.m. on our third day of marriage—one of us very happy to be there and the other wondering if he would ever get to sleep in again! That's a fun memory!

We all started out on our journey of marriage with high hopes, big expectations, and a strong commitment. Along the way, we can lose some of the spark and excitement—sometimes we merely go through the motions, other times are difficult and challenging, some days are busy and hurried. Like the Israelites, we tend to forget.

It's good for us to remember. And as we remember, not only do we laugh and enjoy our early days of marriage, we also celebrate God's faithfulness and goodness in our lives and our marriage.

> The heart of marriage is memories; and if the two of
> you happen to have the same ones and can savor your
> reruns, then your marriage is a gift.
>
> —Bill Cosby, *Love and Marriage*

12

WHAT DO YOU EXPECT?

CHALLENGE 12

What different expectations create challenges
in your marriage?

Hope deferred makes the heart sick, but a longing ful-
filled is a tree of life.

—*Proverbs 13:12*

In our early years of marriages, we were very unaware of the
impact of expectations on our marriage. And yet expectations exist everywhere. We had expectations about everything:
spending and saving money, leisure time, friendships, vacations,
sex, conversations, buying cars—you name it, and expectations
were in play.

When two people come together in marriage, they bring
with them a world of different experiences. Our expectations

come from the families we were raised in, the churches we've attended, the impact of media, our unique cultures, and so much more. Those expectations aren't right or wrong, but they must be spoken and understood. If not, we end up with unmet expectations and then disappointment sets in. When this gap gets created, we must work hard to prevent discouragement, resentment, or bitterness from growing.

Often expectations fall into one of the following categories: unknown, unspoken, or unrealistic. An unknown expectation is something we are unaware of that we carry with us, and it's "hardwired" inside. These often develop from how we saw our parents interact, and we've "inherited" them. We learn styles of relating from what our parents did or didn't do, and we don't realize the impact of these unmet expectations until something feels different in our marriage. Marital roles (housekeeping, paying bills, etc.) often fall into this category.

Sometimes we are aware of our expectations, but we choose not to speak of them. Unspoken expectations can also create difficulty in our marriages. We may think our spouse should know what we want or what we're thinking, even though we know full well that we can't read each other's minds. In those times, we may get angry with our spouse for not knowing what we need—even though we know we're not being sensible.

Finally, there are unrealistic expectations. These can be the most tricky to see. When we begin to compare our marriages to others, it's easy to develop unrealistic expectations by thinking our marriage should look like a friend's or we should be able to do the same things they do. Also, unrealistic expectations are often couched with global terms, such as "always" and "never" ("we should never fight," or "you're always late"). Ultimately, unrealistic expectations happen when we are looking for our spouse or our marriage to fill something that our spouse or marriage is not capable of filling.

Remember, expectations aren't a problem in our marriages. They're actually the playground where hope and dreams can grow. They become problems only when they are unknown to us, they're unspoken, or they're unrealistic—and those lead to unmet expectations. As we become aware of our expectations and discuss them with each other, we can narrow the gap that unmet expectations can create, and in doing so we increase our connection, satisfaction, and intimacy. Here's a practical step for today's question: Spend some time considering where expectations have created challenges in your marriage. It may be helpful to use the three categories of unknown, unspoken, or unrealistic. Block out some time this week and identify these expectations so they don't continue to trip you up in your journey toward intimacy.

> The wider the gap between what we expect and the reality of what we experience, the greater the potential for discouragement and fatigue.
> —Gary Smalley, *Making Love Last Forever*

13

EYES THAT ARE WATCHING

CHALLENGE 13

What does your marriage communicate about love and intimacy to those people who are closest to you?

One generation will commend your works to another; they will tell of your mighty acts. They speak of the glorious splendor of your majesty, and I will meditate on your wonderful works.

—Psalm 145:4–5

I recently had a conversation with my college-age son about love and dating and marriage. In the midst of the conversation, this comment was made: "Dad, it seems like most of the romance of relationships happens before marriage. I mean, I don't see many married couples who look like they enjoy each other. They seem to just go through the motions, kind of like business partners. It looks like the fun and creative date nights are replaced with dinner and a movie." And then he asked me this question: "Dad, when was the last night you planned a great and fun and creative date night with Mom?"

Ouch!

Whether I like it or not, my children are learning a lot about love and intimacy from me. Not from what I say or write about it but from how I live—especially with their mother. I can't hide from the eyes that watch me closest. Sometimes my behavior exposes my anger. Sometimes it reveals my selfishness. Often it shows my apathy and laziness.

All of our marriages are speaking volumes to our children and family and friends. Others see in us a picture of what we really believe about love and marriage, by the way we interact with each other. As I write these words, I'm reminded of Jesus' words in John 13:35: "This is how everyone will recognize that you are my disciples—when they see the love you have for each other."

It's often the little and simple things that best communicate our love: holding hands, big hugs, a tender kiss, saying "I love you," complimenting each other, smiling, and laughing together. These actions between a husband and wife display more than simply living together "kind of like business partners," as my son observed. But having great "fun and creative date nights" is also important. Josh's observation is valid for many marriages. We often do our "best date nights" before marriage, and we get into the rut of "dinner and movie date nights" after marriage. Or at times, we've ignored date nights altogether in the midst of our busy calendar or tight budget or unresolved issues.

It doesn't have to be that way. The antidote is intentionality. And our marriages are always worth our intentional energy. So what is your marriage communicating? What are your simple interactions with each other saying about love? Are there some things you would like to change? When was the last time you had a great fun and creative date night?

In our marriage we tell the next generation what sex and marriage and fidelity look like to Christians. We are prophets, for better and for worse, of the future of Christian marriage.

—Evelyn and James Whitehead, *A Sense of Sexuality*

14

NATURAL BEAUTY

CHALLENGE 14

What are some things you can enjoy doing together outside?

The earth is the LORD's, and everything in it, the world,
and all who live in it.

—*Psalm 24:1*

The early days of spring are a time of new life and a lot of
movement, especially after a long winter. In our neighborhood, it seems that everybody gets outside to enjoy the beauty
of creation: bike riding, hiking, picnics! Those all sound good
to me. I also see other neighbors outside: mulching the flower
beds, power raking the yard, and cleaning out the garage. That
doesn't sound as good!

It really is a great time of the year to get outside and
enjoy some beautiful days and comfortable nights. But there's
more opportunity outside than just fun. It can also lead us to

worship. As the Book of Genesis teaches us, God is the great creator. When He created Eden, it was a perfect and beautiful place for Adam and Eve to enjoy together. Throughout the Bible, there are passages that remind us of His greatness in creation (Psalm 24:1–2, Psalm 65:5–13, Psalm 104).

For some of us, being outside helps us worship God in a fresh way. We see His power, majesty, creativity, and beauty all around. For those people, it's easy to worship God while watching a sunset or enjoying a gentle stream flowing over rocks or hearing birds singing early in the morning. For others of us, we can be so busy that we miss seeing His handiwork in creation. If you're like that, try to take some time in the near future and enjoy the outdoors in a different way. Look around. Listen. Take a deep breath. You may be surprised at how near God is!

Maybe it's as simple as this: Go for a late-night walk in your neighborhood this weekend together. As you walk, talk about other things you can do as a couple outdoors. And enjoy the stroll—in the cool of the day—as you walk under the loving and creative hand of our good God.

If I believe in God's Son and bear in mind that He became man, all creatures will appear a hundred times more beautiful to me than before. Then I will properly appreciate the sun, the moon, the stars, trees, apples, pears, as I reflect that He is Lord over and the center of all things.

—Martin Luther, *Luther's Works*

15

SPEAKING WORDS OF LOVE

CHALLENGE 15

What are some ways you verbalize your love to your spouse? What words do you like to hear from your spouse?

Pleasant words are a honeycomb, sweet to the soul and healing to the bones.

—*Proverbs 16:24*

Several thousand years ago, the world's wisest man wrote these words, "The tongue has the power of life and death" (Proverbs 18:21). The third chapter of the Book of James speaks about the damage that our words can do. As we get older, we realize that the nursery rhyme "Sticks and stones may break my bones, but words will never hurt me" was wrong. Especially in our marriages, most of us would prefer sticks and stones over harmful words!

We all know that words can hurt, and how we use them really matters. Often in times of tension in a marriage, words become the strongest weapon we use against each other. But words should primarily be about encouragement, love, and affirmation. When we choose our words wisely and use them frequently, intimacy in our marriage can grow.

How we use our words is sometimes a gender-related issue. Generally speaking, women are more verbal than men. I've watched many men become paralyzed trying to find the right words to say during a counseling session when asked a specific question by their wives. Their silence in that moment is often interpreted as apathy or guilt or anger, when it's often simply a man searching for the "right" words to say in that moment. For some of us, learning to speak some very simple phrases can be a great value in our marriage. For example:

- I love you.
- I'm sorry.
- Let's hang out.
- I miss you.
- I miss us.
- You look great!
- I love being with you.
- Please forgive me.
- I really like being with you.
- Whoops! My bad.
- You're the best.

- I respect you.
- I've been selfish.
- Hurry home!
- We need to talk.

When we started the 50 Fridays Marriage Challenge, we committed to intentionally growing intimacy in our marriage. Try this, this week: Take a few minutes separately and write out words that you enjoy hearing from your spouse. Then come together and take a few minutes and share these words.

Another way to do that well is to let your words be life-giving to your spouse. How often are you speaking words that encourage and build up your spouse? Are you intentional in growing a vocabulary that communicates love and respect? As you're thinking about this topic, read Ephesians 4:15 together and let Paul's words be your guide to growing in "speaking the truth in love" to each other.

> What you say to your partner and how you say it, is the single most important influence on your relationship. Your love life will sink or swim according to how well you communicate.
>
> —Drs. Les and Leslie Parrott, *Love Talk*

16

GET INSPIRED

CHALLENGE 16

*Name several couples whose marriage relationship you
admire. What things do you see in them that
you desire to imitate?*

Let the wise listen and add to their learning, and let
the discerning get guidance.

—*Proverbs 1:5*

Make a list together of four to five couples you admire. It may
be your parents or other family members. It could be friends
or neighbors. Maybe it's someone from church or from a small
group. Maybe it's just a marriage that you've watched from a
distance. What is it in their marriage that you admire? What
ways of relating can you and your spouse imitate?

Sometimes we look at the *things* other people have, and

we want those *things*. A bigger house. A different car. Or we compare what we *think* their marriage or family is like and decide that theirs is better than ours. That's not a good way to look at others. But there is a way to look at other marriages and gain inspiration and wisdom. Looking and listening to how another couple relates can inspire conversations about how we would like to grow and change in some important areas. As you talk about the things you admire and respect in their marriages, consider some of these areas:

- How does the husband love his wife?
- How does the wife respect her husband?
- How do they show their affection when they're together?
- How do they speak about each other?
- What values do they embrace?
- In what ways do you see them serve others?
- What habits do they practice?
- Where do you see their faith expressed together?
- What do they seem to enjoy doing together?

Beware: this exercise can create a spirit of jealousy or discontent or even an unhealthy fantasy as you look at another couple's marriage. That's why you have to remember that this question is not about comparison. It's about learning from and dreaming together. As you look at and listen to their marriages, talk about what you want to see in your marriage.

Here's another idea: as you find a marriage that you really value and appreciate, take a risk and see if they might be willing to get together for a conversation one night. Several years ago, we had a young married couple ask us if we could come to their house for dessert one night and let them ask us some questions about our marriage. We discovered that this couple had identified several marriages they wanted to learn from and they had created twenty questions to ask each couple. This simple investment was invaluable to their marriage.

So the next time you see a marriage that looks good and strong, look for ways that you can grow from it.

The great secret of a successful marriage is to treat all disasters as incidents and none of the incidents as disasters.

—Harold Nicholson, quoted in
601 Quotes about Marriage and Family

17

A PERSONAL INVITATION

CHALLENGE 17
Where do you sense God is inviting you to grow or change?
What are some specific ways we can pray for each other?

And this is my prayer: that your love may abound
more and more in knowledge and depth of insight, so
that you may be able to discern what is best and may
be pure and blameless until the day of Christ, filled
with the fruit of righteousness that comes through
Jesus Christ—to the glory and praise of God.

—*Philippians 1:9–11*

Growth is a big topic in our world. We want to see our financial investments *grow* so we can be prepared for retirement one
day. We work hard to grow in our careers and skills so we can
advance into the role we want to have in our job. We want

our kids to grow and be exposed to many opportunities. And growth is even more important in our faith journey, both individually and together in our marriage.

A commitment to spiritual growth is not always easy, because growth means change, and change is difficult. However, growth means we are living, really living, as the life of Christ is reproduced in our own lives. As we live in this world, spiritual growth will always be part of our journey. And on that journey we need others who are cheering for us as we grow, others who are praying for us as we allow Christ to be formed in us.

In the context of our marriages, we are to be each other's biggest encouragers. One of the most simple and profound ways to encourage each other in spiritual growth is to pray specifically for each other. To be that to each other, we need to know the place where God is inviting our spouse to grow in order to faithfully and regularly pray for each other. As you talk together this week, spend some time discussing some specific places in each of your lives where you would like to grow spiritually. It could be in the area of Bible study, prayer, journaling, talking about faith with friends, getting involved in a service opportunity, or laying aside some habit.

As you talk about an area where you desire growth, also spend some time this week not only praying *for* your spouse but also praying *with* your spouse. If this is not a regular exercise for the two of you, then take the risk and pray together at least once this week. Praying together requires a posture of humility, trust, and vulnerability. It's in those moments that we can experience—together—our great need to surrender all that we have to the One whose ways are higher, whose wisdom is wiser, whose love is richer, and whose plan is better. And that's a posture that helps us grow.

> Prayer is as natural an expression of faith as breathing is of life.
>
> —Jonathan Edwards, eighteenth-century
> American theologian and pastor,
> *The Works of President Edwards*

18

LET'S HAVE SOME FUN!

CHALLENGE 18
*What would a great date night look like? Be specific: from
how it begins, to what you'll do together, to how it ends!*

Many waters cannot quench love; rivers cannot wash
it away.

—*Song of Solomon 8:7a*

What comes to your mind when you hear the phrase "date
night"? A nice restaurant? The symphony? A ball game? A
movie? Dancing? A picnic?

It's easy for our date nights to fall into a routine, but date
nights can be a great opportunity to spark our intimacy and
recalibrate our marriage. Often when we are planning a date,
we work hard to think about what our spouse would enjoy—
and rightly so. I'm not much of a symphony guy, but Lora

really enjoys an evening like that. One Christmas I surprised her with tickets to Handel's *Messiah*, and it was a blast!

But at times I've missed out on making a fun date-night memory that we could enjoy because I was afraid that Lora might not like it (for example, a table for two at a monster truck rally!). So what if you were to plan a date night that you knew you would enjoy? At first read, that sounds selfish. But it actually could be a way to invite your spouse into *your* world of interest and fun, especially if you both planned a night like that.

Spend some time dreaming and planning what *your* perfect date night would look like. Be very specific with your answer: from how it begins, to where you would go and what you would do, to how it ends! Don't be shy. This is a great opportunity to make a memory for your marriage.

Be creative.

Be honest.

And beware: there's a good chance the two date nights will be very different! And that's okay. After all, men and women really are different. It might be a sporting event one weekend and a parade of homes the next. Dinner could be a picnic on one date and a quaint, white linen tablecloth restaurant on the next. One of the joys of marriage is learning how to enjoy our spouse's preferences and interests and desires, even when entirely different from our own.

After you've spent some time sharing your answers with each other, grab your calendars and put those two unique date nights on the calendars for some time in the near future. And then have fun on your dates!

A successful marriage is one in which you fall in love many times, always with the same person.

—D. W. McLaughlin, as quoted in
Practical Proverbs and Wacky Wit

19

THE LANGUAGES OF LOVE

CHALLENGE 19

What are some behaviors your spouse does
that help you feel loved?

And over all these virtues put on love, which binds
them all together in perfect unity.

—*Colossians 3:14*

In 1992, a marriage counselor published a book that docu-
mented a pattern he had observed in counseling couples.
He noticed that every person seemed to have a main way of
expressing and interpreting love, and he categorized them
into five different categories. For more than twenty years this
book has remained a bestseller and has been used by count-
less people to understand how couples give and receive love.
This book, *The 5 Love Languages*, by Dr. Gary Chapman, has

sold millions of copies with a simple yet profound message: we need to know how our spouses receive love in order to love them well. He identifies these five languages: words of affirmation, quality time, receiving gifts, acts of service, and physical touch; and he notes that most of us have one or two primary love languages.

Some of us receive love through words of affirmation. Compliments, encouragement, and affirmation fill our love tank like nothing else. For people with this love language, insults and negative words can create great pain and hurt.

Quality time is the second love language. In our early years of marriage, Lora would often want to go on walks just to spend time together. For me, walking seemed like a chore or exercise, and I would often be dismissive of her desire. Years later, as we discovered the love languages, her desire for a walk was a simple way of spending quality time together.

Some people experience love from their spouse through receiving gifts. This love language is usually more connected to thoughtfulness than expensive gifts. For these people, gifts are a tangible symbol of love, and so the price and size of the gift are not as important as what it represents. A single flower, a favorite candy bar, or even a handmade craft often communicate love.

The fourth love language is acts of service. This language is often centered around household chores such as cooking, cleaning, paying bills, picking up laundry, vacuuming, oil changes, and other daily activities. Although these things could be seen as merely chores, they can be done with a posture and spirit that expresses love to those with this love language.

Finally, there's the love language of physical touch. Don't limit this language to sexual touch only. Physical touch communicates love in a powerful way through hugging, holding hands, foot rubs, massages, and much more.

Some of us have known about Dr. Chapman's five love languages for a long time, and this is a good review and chance for us to evaluate how well we are loving our spouse in his or her love language. For others this may be new information (if so, this is a great book to read together). Learning each other's love language and expressing love through it helps our love grow, and in doing so we enjoy our marriages even more.

Love is something you do for someone else, not something you do for yourself.

—Gary Chapman, *The 5 Love Languages*

20

LISTENING WELL

CHALLENGE 20

What are some practical ways to listen better to your spouse?

Everyone should be quick to listen, slow to speak, and
slow to become angry.

—*James 1:19b*

When I was a young boy, my mom would often say, "God gave
you two ears and one mouth so you can listen twice as much
as you speak." Decades later, there are times when I'm not sure
that I've fully grasped the wisdom of that adage—especially
when it comes to listening well in my marriage. Lora and I
have worked hard to develop healthy communication patterns,
and yet it's very easy to relapse to poor ways of relating. Generally, when our communication breaks down, it's because one
or both of us have stopped listening well (yes, usually me!).

Developing good listening skills is really important. At times it seems that listening is more important than even what we say. Here's a challenge for today: work together as a couple and create your own list of practical ways to listen better to each other. Here are a few simple thoughts that might help get you started on your list:

1. Only one person speaks at a time; therefore the other person is focused on listening.

2. When listening, make eye contact with your spouse. Focus. Acknowledge that you're listening by nodding your head or offering an "uh-huh" from time to time.

3. Remember the four *don'ts*: Don't interrupt. Don't rebut. Don't judge. Don't shut down.

4. Summarize what you've heard. After your spouse finishes talking, summarize what you've heard him or her say. For example: "So what I heard you say was . . ."

5. Acknowledge feelings. Good listening is not only about the facts; it's also about acknowledging the emotion in the conversation. For example: "It seems like you're really sad about . . ."

6. Be curious. Ask open-ended questions. Remember the most powerful three words of listening: "Tell me more."

Final thought: Learning to listen well is an important part of any strong marriage. If we don't listen well, we may miss what our spouse is trying to say. Often we listen in order to "pick a fight" or to "form our response," and we can miss the real intent of our spouse. "Big picture listening" is learning to hear what's really being said, not just focusing on a word or a phrase that triggers something in us. Diane Sollee of the Marriage Institute illustrates it this way:

"Aoccdrnig to rscheearch at Cmabrigde Uinervtisy, it deosn't mttaer in what oredr the ltteers in a wrod are, the olny iprmoetnt tihng is taht the frist and lsat ltteer be at the rghit pclae. The rset can be a toatl mses and you can sitll raed it wouthit a porbelm. Tihs is bcuseae the huamn mnid deos not raed ervey lteter by istlef, but the wrod as a wlohe. Amzanig huh?"

She continues, "It makes me think we should be able to apply this principle to marital communication. Try to listen for the meaning instead of nit-picking at the fine points."

Well said, Diane!

Being heard is so close to being loved that for the average person, they are almost indistinguishable.

—David Augsburger, *Caring Enough to Hear and Be Heard*

21

SEXUAL INTIMACY DO'S AND DON'TS

CHALLENGE 21

What specific changes would you like to see that could help grow a more intimate, pleasurable, and satisfying sex life?

Marriage should be honored by all, and the marriage bed kept pure.

—*Hebrews 13:4a*

God made sex and therefore it is good. And yet one of the most common areas of conflict in marriages is the area of sexual intimacy. As we talk with couples, we often discover that many couples struggle to communicate their desires and longings. It seems easier to complain and be frustrated with our spouse than to engage in healthy communication about what we would like to see change.

We all know that good communication is an important foundation for a great marriage. We understand that we need to work hard to communicate about children, money, in-laws, vacations, and spiritual growth. We realize that we need to share our thoughts, feelings, and dreams with each other. It seems that we can talk about our finances, our vacation plans, our children's schedules, and upcoming holiday travel. But when it comes to the topic of sexual intimacy, many couples struggle to have meaningful and intentional conversations that help grow their sex lives. It's even easier to talk with a good friend than our spouse.

There may be a number of reasons why it's difficult to talk with our spouse about sexual intimacy: it might be fear or shame or unresolved tension or a low-grade anger. Whatever the reason, there comes a time when we need to move beyond the barriers and have an important conversation, and today's question is a good starting place. Here are a few guidelines to help this conversation go well:

1. Let your spouse know that you'd like to talk about sexual intimacy and decide together when and where is a good time to have this conversation.

2. Speak for yourself and be honest with your feelings, thoughts, and desires.

3. Strive to really listen to your spouse. Ask questions to clarify what he or she is saying.

4. Remember this is only one conversation; you don't have to solve everything right now. There will be time for more discussion.
5. Pick one thing that you can agree on and decide how you can act on something specific and together.

Here's another way to talk about your sex life. Take turns completing the following sentences:

- In leading up to sexual intimacy, I like for you to . . .
- During sex, I like for you to . . .
- During sex, I don't like when you . . .
- After sex, I would like to . . .

Remember, God made sex and it's His idea; therefore, it is good. So talk about some ways that you can enjoy His good gift.

Should lovemaking within marriage be considered a fundamentally spiritual activity? I believe the answer is an unqualified yes.

—C. J. Mahaney, *Sex, Romance, and the Glory of God*

HIGHS AND LOWS

CHALLENGE 22
What was the best thing that happened to you
this past week? What was your greatest challenge?

A friend loves at all times, and a brother is born for
adversity.

—Proverbs 17:17

If you were to listen in to the Helton family dinner-table
conversations, you would often hear Lora ask our children
this question: *So what was your high and low today?* It's a simple
question that invites our kids to share the best of their day and
the hardest part of their day. The answers are often quick and
at times somewhat generic, but they provide a framework for
deeper conversations at other times.

This week's question is a "high/low" one. It gives an

opportunity to make sure we really are aware of what's going on in each other's lives—even in the midst of crazy schedules! It's good to know the highlight of each other's days and to be able to celebrate the fun and exciting part of life. It might be something as simple as a new restaurant or a funny story for the day. At the same time, it's great to know what challenges your spouse faced—a tough day with one of the children or a disappointing situation at work.

But knowing the highs and lows in each other's life is just the beginning. The next step is to move from knowing to engaging and caring. In other words, we're not just swapping facts about our days; rather, we're striving to understand more about what our spouse is thinking and feeling. There are many ways we can show we care. Sometimes it's by acting on what we've heard. Sometimes just listening with compassion and empathy shows we care.

But all of the time, we can show our care by praying with each other. So often, it's easy to pray *for* each other. But there's something rich that happens when we pray *with* each other. Praying with each other provides the opportunity to hear our spouse speak our name to our Father. Praying together recalibrates us and reminds us that a great plan is unfolding, even if we don't see it. Praying together allows us to speak of our need to be dependent upon One who is much greater than our highest of highs or lowest of lows.

As you answer this week's question, spend time together in prayer, giving thanks for the excitements of this past week and asking God for direction and wisdom in the areas that are challenging.

Shared joy is a doubled joy; shared sorrow is half a sorrow.

—Old Swedish proverb

BUCKET LIST

CHALLENGE 23

Name something you've never done but would like to try.
Why does it appeal to you? What's kept you from trying it?

Have I not commanded you? Be strong and coura-
geous. Do not be terrified; do not be discouraged, for
the LORD your God will be with you wherever you go.

—*Joshua 1:9*

Our oldest son, Josh, is always up for an adventure. A few years
ago it was skydiving. The following summer he spent a month
in Africa and then bungee jumped from the highest platform
in North America! The next year he and some friends planned
a trip across America to raise money for an orphanage in
Kenya—and they did it by hitchhiking! He has one of those

personalities that love taking risks. By the time he's our age, today's question may be hard for him to answer—he will have tried it all!

Although most of us may not be dreaming about extreme (or crazy) activities like Josh, many of us have something we have considered doing but have never gotten around to. Today's question could lead to some fun discussion—or maybe even a new adventure for one or both of you, such as repelling, running a marathon, parasailing, or bungee jumping. Maybe each of you needs to create a "bucket list." I'm not sure where that phrase originated, but the simple definition is "a list of things to do before you kick the bucket." It's not necessarily the most sensitive language, but you quickly understand what it means. Jeff's eighty-five-year-old dad recently announced that he would like to skydive with Josh. When he discovered that he had some medical conditions that wouldn't allow him to jump from a plane, he changed his wish to riding in a hot air balloon. That's how a bucket list works!

After you've created and shared your individual bucket list, you can create your marriage bucket list. Maybe there's something you've always wanted to try together but haven't. It could be ballroom dance lessons, traveling overseas, creative dates, or developing a new hobby. Try this exercise sometime this week: What are ten things that together you could put on your marriage bucket list? Dream big as you make this list. We encourage you to actually create the list and write it down. From time to time pull the list out and see what you can plan to accomplish, how to make it happen, and when you'll do so.

Hey, we're not getting any younger, so let's take some risks and see what we learn and what memories we make together.

Great love and great achievements involve great risks.

—Anonymous

24

TIME WELL SPENT

CHALLENGE 24

*On an average week, how much time do
you and your spouse spend together in meaningful
and connecting conversation?*

Be very careful, then, how you walk—not as unwise
but as wise, making the most of every opportunity, because the days are evil. Therefore do not be foolish, but
understand what the LORD's will is.

—Ephesians 5:15–17

Almost every woman and man would admit that good communication is essential to growing an intimate marriage. But
it's amazing how easy it is to get into poor communication
patterns and habits—especially when there are younger children around the house. It's possible for a marriage to go several

weeks without any intentional conversation. It's not good, but it's possible.

Here's an exercise for you to do: evaluate your checkbook and your calendar. It's been said that you can tell a lot about what a person values by looking at their checkbook register and their calendar. It makes sense: where you spend your money and where you spend your time are good indicators of what you value.

WOW! That hurts a little when I looked at my checkbook and my calendar for the past month. If it wasn't for Mother's Day in May, I would be in the zero column on that evaluation. It's not that Lora and I haven't spent some time together—I'm sure we have (I've even asked her!). I'm not suggesting that it requires money and planning to have quality time together. I would much rather see couples who develop a rhythm of intentional daily conversation instead of spending big dollars on extravagant dates but don't really connect. Yet there's something to be said for evaluating your intentionality of connecting.

Many months ago, when we started on the 50 Fridays journey, we said that "we desired to be committed to growing authentic and intentional marriages." At the heart of that commitment is time spent together talking, dreaming, and connecting. Look at the rhythm of your life: Where do you need to make some tweaks and adjustments? How can you add some level of intentionality to your marriage? What can you put on your calendar that will help you connect?

We know that spending time together is important. For

some of us we need to step it up. Here are some ideas to get you started. I'm sure you can do much better.

- Have lunch together on a regular basis.
- Go for a short walk—night walks can be fun and romantic.
- Work together (the dishes, weeding the flower bed, etc.). It may not sound like quality time, but it can be.
- Don't talk on your cell phone when you're in the car together (that one is really for me!).
- Turn off the radio and just talk in the car.
- Take showers together.
- Work out a deal with another couple to have them watch your kids overnight so you can have a romantic evening alone; then you watch their children for them.
- Take turns planning a date night.
- Develop a hobby together: tennis, cooking, biking, etc.

Be creative. Look for ways to spend intentional time together growing intimacy in your marriage.

Married life isn't a time for settling down but for growth, for doing new things. With each passing year a growing couple will actively look for new and different things they can do together.

—Dale Evans Rogers, *God in the Hard Times*

RUN YOUR RACE

CHALLENGE 25

How do you need to "run the race of faith" differently?
Where is God inviting you to grow and change?

It is for freedom that Christ has set us free. Stand firm,
then, and do not let yourselves be burdened again by a
yoke of slavery.

—*Galatians 5:1*

Psalm 119:32 says, "I run in the path of your commands, for you
have set my heart free." Freedom is such a great gift and very
worthy of being celebrated. When we are free, we respond with
great joy—for the psalmist his response was to run! That's why
we often talk about running the race of faith. In Galatians 5,
Paul encourages us to stand firm and to keep running a good
race in light of the freedom that Christ has given us.

But Paul also understands that there are situations and relationships that can prevent us from running our race well. In verse 7 he asks this question: "You were running a good race. Who cut in on you to keep you from obeying the truth?" In the race of the Christian life, there are distractions and obstacles that can cause us to stop running well. When that happens, we find ourselves feeling trapped or confused. We start getting off course. We sense that something is not right. We feel burdened—or at times, even enslaved. When that happens in our personal lives, it impacts our marriages as well.

The writer of Hebrews also uses the race metaphor to describe the Christian life in Hebrews 12:1–3 and gives some practical thoughts on how to run well. Read this passage together. Notice his simple but important encouragements:

- Throw off anything that hinders us from running well.
- Beware of how sin trips us up in the race of faith.
- Keep running—run with perseverance.
- Keep your eyes focused on Jesus.

When we get off course in our race or when we get lazy and don't run our race of faith very well, we can get back on track quickly through confession and repentance. Confession is merely agreeing with what God already knows about us. And repentance is simply changing the direction in which we're going.

Running well in our individual race of faith empowers us to love each other more fully and live more freely. Our freedom in Christ is a great gift that we can enjoy. Spend some time sharing how your race is going. If there are things that are hindering your freedom, share those and pray for each other. If you're running well, then celebrate that together and keep running your race well.

Please root from my heart all those things which I have cherished so long and which have become a very part of my living self, so that Thou mayest enter and dwell there without a rival.

—A. W. Tozer, *The Pursuit of God*

26

FINDING YOUR WAY

CHALLENGE 26
*What in your spiritual pathway helps you
experience and love God?*

Jesus replied: "Love the LORD your God with all your
heart and with all your soul and with all your mind."
This is the first and greatest commandment. And the
second is like it: "Love your neighbor as yourself."

—*Matthew 22:37–39*

Almost every morning, Lora rises early and heads downstairs
where her morning routine begins. As the coffeepot brews
her morning energy drink, she finishes making school lunches
or puts away the last of the now dry dishes from the previous
night's dinner. Once her first cup of coffee is in hand, Lora
makes her way to the living room, lights a single candle, and

sits on the couch with her Bible and journal in hand. For the next thirty minutes or so, Lora will be in communion with God through reading, reflection, study, prayer, meditation, and journaling. She has often said that when she misses her morning routine (which she rarely does) her day is out of sorts. It's Lora's pathway to spending time with God.

My pathway looks significantly different, and for years I felt like my way was inferior. After all, most of the Sunday school teachers of my youth taught that real Christians have a quiet time that looks like Lora's! However, I commune with God far more easily by having deep conversations with a trusted friend or discussing something new that I'm learning.

Each of us is uniquely created by God with different personalities and temperaments. We also have different ways of experiencing and encountering God. Gary Thomas calls the way we encounter God our "pathway" in his book *Sacred Pathways*. He says that our pathway frees us to fully worship and love God in the way that we were created. Thomas identifies the following nine pathways:

1. Naturalists: Loving God Outdoors
2. Sensates: Loving God with the Senses
3. Traditionalists: Loving God through Ritual and Symbol
4. Ascetics: Loving God in Solitude and Simplicity
5. Activists: Loving God through Confrontation
6. Caregivers: Loving God by Loving Others

7. Enthusiasts: Loving God with Mystery and Celebration
8. Contemplatives: Loving God through Adoration
9. Intellectuals: Loving God with the Mind

When we look at Thomas's list of pathways, Lora is a combination of the ascetics and the naturalists. One of her favorite places of communion with God is walking by herself on the beach, enjoying God's creativity majesty and beauty. I'm more of an activist and am energized by and aware of God's presence in times of moving things forward and working through challenging situations. When you look at the list, which pathway best describes your preference toward encountering God? Many of us have more than one pathway, and we may use different pathways in different seasons of our lives. These pathways cannot replace the need for time in the Bible or time in prayer. Rather, they help us understand the ways and places in which our walk with Christ can grow richer and deeper.

More than likely, you and your spouse have different pathways. It's really helpful to understand how each of you best encounters God. The goal is not to develop the same pathway, but rather to understand and appreciate another way you're different!

If you are in a spiritual malaise, it might be that you just need a change in your spiritual diet.

—Gary Thomas, *Sacred Pathways*

CHEAP DATE

CHALLENGE 27
*If you could spend only ten dollars on a date night,
what would you do?*

For our boast is this, the testimony of our conscience,
that we behaved in the world with simplicity and
godly sincerity, not by earthly wisdom but by the
grace of God, and supremely so toward you.
—*2 Corinthians 1:12, ESV*

I have a confession: I'm a Groupon groupie.

Groupon is a website that offers a deal-of-the-day coupon
that you can purchase for stuff to do, see, eat, or buy in your
city. At first I was skeptical, until I saw a fifty-dollar gift card
for one of our favorite restaurants for only twenty-five dollars!
Then I was sold. I love a date night at a good restaurant, especially if the meal is 50 percent off!

I think all of us would agree that regular date nights can be a great asset to our marriages. Whether we go out for a nice dinner or catch a fun movie or go to another favorite activity, date nights are a great escape and a fun time. But there's another kind of date night that is beneficial for our marriages: those nights when we just spend time connecting, talking, and dreaming: no big activity required, just being together. Those nights don't require spending a lot of money. We know that the point of a good date night is not the money we spend but the time we spend together.

Two quick examples: Chuck and Jean were some friends in Chicago who lived a block from a small, family-owned diner. In the early days of their marriage, they decided that every Tuesday night they would walk to the diner and share a piece of homemade pie and two cups of coffee while catching up with each other. The last time I saw Chuck he told me that for more than thirty-four years that has continued to be their Tuesday night routine, with few exceptions! When Mark and Susan had their fourth child, they realized that getting a babysitter and spending money on dinner and a movie was going to put too much strain on their family's budget. So they decided to develop their own "movie theater" in their bonus room. For years, they've had a weekly date night on Thursday evenings in their own home, complete with a "Do Not Disturb" note on the bonus room door that all of their children grew up learning to respect!

So, what if you try this challenge: over the next month or

so, each of you plan a date night, but spend only ten dollars on the date! It's not just a chance to save some money and to be creative, but it might just help you connect with each other in a different way.

> Creating informal rituals when you can connect emotionally is critical in a marriage.
>
> —John Gottman, *The Seven Principles for Making Marriage Work*

CHEERLEADERS

CHALLENGE 28

*Who cheers for your marriage? Who are the encouragers
for you as a husband or a wife?*

Therefore encourage one another and build each
other up, just as in fact you are doing.

—*1 Thessalonians 5:11*

For more than two decades, nine of Lora's girlfriends from her
days at Taylor University converge every other year on someone's house for a long weekend. These few days are packed
with retelling old stories and giving updates on new journeys.
Family pictures provide updates on children who have grown
and transitioned. There are moments of laughter and moments
of tears. There are stories of blessing and brokenness. Stories of
hope and hurt . . . of faith and fear . . . of love and loss.

Updates on their marriages are always a staple item at these reunions. Through vulnerable and transparent sharing, they ultimately have the opportunity to support, confront, and encourage one another as wives. Allowing others to really know what's going on opens the door for growth with one another and in their marriages. When these girls met in the early eighties, none of them knew that God was knitting their hearts together for a lifetime adventure. So much of what they learned then continues to impact them almost three decades later! It's amazing to see them still enjoy a shared faith and values.

Lora and her friends are really blessed. Few of us have maintained friendships with that many people for so many years—especially friendships that encourage us to walk by faith, love our spouses well, and engage the world. And yet we all need relationships like that, whether they're with old or new friends. Our marriages benefit from cheerleaders who encourage us and support us and, at times, challenge us to grow. We may connect with those people through church, shared hobbies, neighborhood gatherings, or a variety of other ways. One of the best and easiest ways we've connected with other couples is through a small group or through an intentional mentoring relationship. Those environments help set up an expectation of authentic sharing and caring.

So who are those people for you? Who is cheering for intentional growth toward intimacy in your marriage? If you're in a season where you're not experiencing this, how could you find another couple to walk with? What would it look like to initiate with someone and spend time together, really getting to know them? As you're discussing today's question, also consider its flip side: Where are you and your spouse the cheerleader for other marriages? Who is a couple that you could intentionally invest in?

That may be the place to start!

A marriage is not a joining of two worlds, but an abandoning of two worlds in order that one new one might be formed.

—Mike Mason, *The Mystery of Marriage*

TELL ME NOW

CHALLENGE 29

If you had only one day left on earth, what would you say to your spouse? What would you want to do with your spouse?

Now listen, you who say, "Today or tomorrow we will go to this or that city, spend a year there, carry on business, and make money." Why, you do not even know what will happen tomorrow. What is your life? You are a mist that appears for a little while and then vanishes. Instead, you ought to say, "If it is the LORD's will, we will live and do this or that."

—*James 4:13–15*

Life is fragile.

Over the past few years, we've seen so many moments that remind us of this simple truth. Shooting tragedies at schools, a movie theater, and in churches have headlined our news. Natural tragedies such as earthquakes, floods, and hurricanes create loss and pain. All of this reminds us that life is fragile. Many of us have experienced the loss of loved ones to cancer, heart disease, or accidents. Through these times of loss, we tend to develop a heightened sense of how quickly this life can end.

But life is fragile not only in times of violence or sickness, but also every day in every situation. None of us is promised tomorrow. And yet . . .

. . . we often live as if life has no end.

. . . we are guilty of withholding love and words until a later time.

. . . we justify holding on to hurts and grudges instead of engaging in conversation.

. . . we live as if we have thousands of tomorrows.

. . . we wait for those tomorrows and we miss our todays.

Obviously we don't need to live with a dark shadow of pending doom hanging over our heads. That's no way to live. But at the same time, we need to acknowledge that many of us have a tendency to postpone, procrastinate, or withhold kindness, love, and good deeds—especially within our marriage. And in light of the truth that we don't know how many days any of us have, the old adage is true: we should live every day as if it were our last. It's not a call to live recklessly. It's a call to be alive! Cherish today. Keep short accounts. Speak words of love. Engage passionately.

And in the end, it's not the years in your life that count. It's the life in your years.

—Abraham Lincoln, *Congressional Record*

30

FAILURE IS NOT FINAL

CHALLENGE 30
How do you handle failure?

Therefore confess your sins to each other and pray for
each other so that you may be healed.

—James 5:16

I hate to fail. Or better stated, I don't like to be a failure.

And yet it happens all the time—or so it seems. I can't get
the Christmas lights to work some years. I didn't get a bill paid
on time. I wasn't able to finish the project I started for work.
And on and on the list goes. Failure seems to happen everywhere. And yet the greatest teacher in my life has been failure.
Every time I "come up short" on what I want to accomplish, I
learn a lesson. Usually that lesson helps me do better the next
time I try that same thing.

I remember the first time I preached a sermon. A professor I had in college was there. Afterward he came up to me and said, "You would be a good actor, but you're not much of a preacher." Talk about feeling like a failure! Wow! The truth is, the sermon wasn't very good. I didn't know what I was doing. But almost thirty years later, that "failure" still drives me to prepare well and to do my best when I'm preaching or speaking somewhere.

That's one way to respond to failure—to work harder when you experience failure. In some situations that's the good response. But in our walk with Christ, "working harder" doesn't really work. In our walk with Jesus, there are times when we feel like a failure. Honestly, there are times when we fail and fail big. The Bible is filled with stories of saints who failed God. I think of Peter denying Jesus. Big failure. I think of David committing adultery and murder. Huge failure. And yet God used those moments in both of their lives to grow them up and remind them that He is *always* bigger than our failures. Their response was not to work harder—it was to trust more.

In our walk with Christ, trusting the grace of Jesus is critical. It takes some of us decades to understand that. Today I'm so thankful for God's grace. When we fall, He is quick to forgive, restore, and grow us up from our failures. In our marriages, learning to speak of our failures and extending grace to each other allow us to live openly instead of hiding. As we develop the willingness to confess our failures—and our sins—to each other, we experience grace at a deeper level. Ultimately our failures are never the last word. God's grace is.

Never let the fear of striking out get in your way.

—George Herman "Babe" Ruth, as quoted in
Bobby Bowden on Leadership, by Pat Williams

DOLLARS AND SENSE

CHALLENGE 31

How's your financial situation? How are you doing in
saving, giving, and spending your money?
Do you have a good financial plan?

The plans of the diligent lead to profit as surely as haste leads to poverty.

—*Proverbs 21:5*

Money is an essential part of lives. Of itself, it's neither good nor bad, but how we use it can bring great joy and fulfillment or create a lot of tension and heartache in our marriages. Research has shown us that money is one of the main areas of conflict in marriage. A recent CNN survey discovered that couples fight twice as much about money as they fight about sex. So being intentional in how we handle our money is important.

We all have heard and know that having a budget is crucial. But I'm amazed at the number of marriages that operate without a budget to help navigate how to use money well. Author and pastor John Maxwell defines a budget as "people telling their money where to go instead of asking where it went." Radio personality Dave Ramsey says that in our budgeting we need to give every dollar a name so we know exactly how we're spending it.

At the most basic level, every marriage needs to have a financial plan that includes how we spend money, save money, and give money. In our early years of marriage, we didn't do a good job of planning how to use money. Part of the reason was that we approached money differently. I came from a family where there was no teaching about money, and using consumer credit was a common way of life. I finished graduate school with more than forty thousand dollars of student loans and a big car payment. Lora, on the other hand, was raised in a missionary family and learned the value of a dollar at a young age. She came into our marriage with a very frugal and "cash only" way of living. Unfortunately, we wasted many years and made some poor financial decisions by not developing an intentional financial plan.

Taking control of your financial situation can actually become a fun process. When a husband and wife begin to dream about where they want to be and develop the self-discipline to get there, working with money can actually become a place of growing in unity. But we have to be on the same page.

We often recommend that couples go through some type of financial training together. One of our favorites is Dave Ramsey's Financial Peace University. This seminar provides practical advice and counsel to help couples begin having conversations about money and develop an intentional plan to achieve financial goals.

Not all of us need financial advice, but all of us need a financial plan. Like any other area in our marriage, good conversation and an intentional strategy help us grow and experience a deeper level of unity and connection. If it's been awhile since you've thoroughly discussed your financial situation, schedule some time this week to look over where you are and to plan what needs to happen next.

> You must gain control over your money or the lack of it will forever control you.
>
> —Dave Ramsey, *Financial Peace Revisited*

DELIGHTING IN
THE DIFFERENCES

CHALLENGE 32

In what way are you and your spouse really different?

How great is the love the Father has lavished on us,
that we should be called children of God! And that is
what we are!

—*1 John 3:1*

Before we were married, Lora and I thought that our marriage
would be conflict-free. After attending a Family Life Marriage
Conference the spring before we were married, we left thinking that married couples tend to fight a lot. We heard a couple
speak during the conference, and they talked about how much
conflict they had in their marriage and how they had to learn
skills to resolve conflict well. They talked about learning to

paraphrase what the other one had said, how to call a time-out when the conflict escalated, and other resolution skills they needed. We really felt sorry for that couple and all of the conflict they had in marriage. We were sure that wouldn't happen to us—after all, we were so similar!

What a joke. We weren't actually that similar. We were simply blind.

Many of us started marriage without considering how different we are. We have so many categories of differences: gender differences, created differences, personality differences, communication-style differences, family-of-origin differences—and that's just naming a few areas. In the early years of marriage, many couples work hard to get rid of the differences. In effect, we often try to become more like each other. "You give a little, and I'll give a little" is the motto of many marriages. It's as if there's an unspoken rule that says we should be alike.

In 1991 Larry Crabb wrote a book titled *Men and Women: Enjoying the Differences*. His premise was pretty simple: we really are different, and we can (and must) learn to enjoy our differences. He says that the biggest reason we struggle to celebrate our spouse's difference ultimately boils down to selfishness. It makes sense. There are times when I would much rather Lora respond the same way I do or think the same way I think. At the core, I'm often lazy and don't want to spend the time talking through something. That's a subtle form of selfishness.

Learning to delight in and enjoy our spouse's differences

is an important part of growing an intimate marriage. Instead of letting your differences lead you to conflict or isolation, look for opportunities to enjoy the differences between the two of you—whether they are little areas or big areas. But be prepared: it will require patience, a sense of humor, and a forgiving spirit! But it's so worth it.

> We have a choice: we can either delight in diversity or destroy distinctions.
> —Dan Allender and Tremper Longman III, *Intimate Allies*

ROCK, PAPER, SCISSORS

CHALLENGE 33
*How do you make a decision when you
disagree on something?*

Two are better than one, because they have a good
return for their labor: if either of them falls down, one
can help the other up. But pity anyone who falls and
has no one to help them up.

—*Ecclesiastes 4:9–10, NIV 2011*

When I was a young boy and my best friend, Mark, and I
couldn't agree on what to do during one of our many summer-
time adventures, we always had a certain way to make a quick
and easy decision: rock, paper, scissors. It was failproof. Whoever
won the best two-out-of-three made the decision for either
fishing or basketball. Imagine my surprise in our first month of

marriage when Lora and I were stuck trying to make a decision and she didn't share my passion for rock, paper, scissors!

Marriage is filled with decisions to be made: budget, leisure time, serving opportunities, friends, in-laws, and housework, to name a few. Sometimes those decisions are easy to discuss and make. At other times we can get stuck because we don't agree on how to move forward. If we don't have an intentional plan for decision-making, default decisions may be made by the more dominant, emotional, or verbal spouse. In the early days of our marriage, I would often "filibuster" an issue by talking so much that Lora would give in to my way just to find peace! The wisdom from Solomon in today's scripture is a strong guideline for decision-making—two really are better than one.

When making a decision becomes challenging, the following questions can be helpful:

1. *What's the real issue here?* It's easy to get stuck in the emotion of the moment and lose sight of the real issue. For example, we may get stuck deciding if our son should play football, when the real issue is a concern for our child's size and safety. Clarifying the issue is a good first step in decision-making.

2. *What are some potential solutions?* Most of us have participated in a brainstorming session where every idea counts. We find that when a couple can brainstorm different solutions for a problem, it frees them to start working together instead of against each other.

3. *How important is this decision really?* Sometimes stopping and looking at the importance of the decision allows one of us to relax and defer. Not every decision that we make in marriage is critical.

4. *Am I really listening to my spouse's point of view?* We work hard to communicate our reasons and thinking for making a decision. Healthy marriages work equally hard to listen to and understand the other person's thoughts and concerns.

5. *Have we prayed together for wisdom about this decision?* Taking time to pray for God's direction and wisdom brings clarity and a good decision. In prayer we have the opportunity to trust God's guidance and goodness in the midst of our confusion. He is faithful to lead us toward His truth.

Decision-making will always be a part of our marriages. Learning to make decisions together helps us develop a deeper connection with each other. Taking time to communicate well always grows us together in a way that rock, paper, scissors just can't do!

Even couples who agree on their decision may not agree about their feelings after the choice has been made. Before, during, and after a decision, it's better if you can make a Connection.

—Tim and Joy Downs, *The Seven Conflicts*

34

SEPARATE AND INTERTWINED

CHALLENGE 34

When you hear the phrase "one flesh,"
how does that describe your marriage?

For this reason a man will leave his father and mother and be united to his wife, and they will become one flesh.

The man and his wife were both naked, and they felt no shame.

—*Genesis 2:24–25*

Let's do a little math. What's 1 + 1? Obviously the answer is 2, except when we're talking about marriage, and then God's math for our marriage creates an equation that looks like this:

1 + 1 = 1. At many weddings, we see this illustrated by the lighting of the unity candle and the "blowing out" of the two individual candles. I love the story of the two older men talking at a wedding reception. One of them said, "The pastor said that the two became one during the ceremony, but during their first year of marriage they'll find out which one."

When we were married we had the unity candle, but we forgot to blow out our own candles and so we had all three candles burning. Although an accident, I think it better represents the miracle and mystery (and math) of oneness in marriage. Some marriages, in an attempt to be one, create a new math that can be written like this: ? + ? = 1 or ⅔ + ⅓ = 1. In math terms, we try to get the right sum to the equation by adjusting the addends. When that happens, we create a marriage where neither husband nor wife is *fully* present, and patterns of mind reading, caretaking, and even codependence can develop. At its worst, one spouse may completely lose his or her voice, and the marriage revolves around what the other spouse wants, needs, and desires.

In a "one flesh" marriage, both husband and wife are fully present and continually choose to grow in their unity and connection over the lifetime of their marriage. They understand the principle of "leave, cleave, and weave" that we see in today's Bible passage. For two to become one, we must *leave* behind our past attitudes, relationships, behaviors, and desires as we enter into this new relationship. In some marriages, parents or previous spouses still have too much influence, and that prevents oneness. We also must *cleave* to our spouse. The idea of cleaving is to be united, but that's not merely a reference to the wedding day. Cleaving is a statement of priority; we cleave as we continually choose our spouse over all others. And finally, we must *weave*. As our marriages grow, our lives become more entwined and connected as we constantly learn how to love and cherish each other. And we do that best when we bring a healthy sense of who we each are individually in Christ, and then fully give of ourselves to each other.

A really good marriage has the feel of a man and woman blending together into natural movement where individuality is obviously present but really isn't the point, something perhaps like dance partners of many years who anticipate each other's steps with practiced ease.

—Larry Crabb, *Enjoying the Difference*

BLESSINGS AND CURSES

CHALLENGE 35

*When you think about the family you were raised in, what
things do you want to carry on into your family?*

This day I call the heavens and the earth as witnesses
against you that I have set before you life and death,
blessings and curses. Now choose life, so that you and
your children may live and that you may love the LORD
your God, listen to His voice, and hold fast to Him.

—*Deuteronomy 30:19–20*

Several years ago, while sitting in a counselor's office, I was
asked to think about the family that I was raised in and how
it had impacted me. The specific question was something like
this: "How did your family bless you? And how did your family curse you?" I wasn't sure that I liked that question. The

blessing part was okay to answer, but talking about how my family cursed me was confusing. It brought to mind some strange movie with voodoo dolls!

But the truth is that all of our families have blessed us and cursed us. For most of us it's not because our parents were wicked, but because they were human. All of us have been raised in a broken and imperfect world. No matter how wonderful our parents were, they were still imperfect and brought their imperfections into their parenting. Acknowledging their humanity and their limitations helps us truly understand some of the things that we may still carry around with us.

For example, in my family, humor was used to cover up pain and to avoid discussing hard issues. In the early years of our marriage, when things would get difficult, I would often make a joke or find a way to laugh off the issue. This may seem like a small area, but it became a way that I avoided much-needed conversations. At the same time, my family's sense of humor has blessed me in many ways. Our home has been richer because of our ability to laugh and to "roll with the punches" on some hard days.

Looking at our families of origin is a great exercise in understanding how generational patterns can develop unknowingly. Counselors will often have couples draw a genogram or a family tree that includes a couple of generations back. In doing this exercise, couples can look for patterns of relating that have developed among grandparents, siblings, and other family members. These patterns often form family rules that we unintentionally learn to live by. Some of these are encouraging and helpful. Some need to be addressed and changed.

The psalmist says in Psalm 16:6 that his "heritage is beautiful" (NASB). As we come to really understand the families we've been raised in and how our lives have been impacted by them, we can join his words and choose life as we begin building the next generation of our family story.

> In every conceivable manner, the family is link to our past, bridge to our future.
>
> —Alex Haley, as quoted in *Real Relationships*,
> by Drs. Les and Leslie Parrott

36

A GOOD APOLOGY

CHALLENGE 36

How are you at apologizing when
you've messed up in your marriage?

Get rid of all bitterness, rage and anger, brawling and
slander, along with every form of malice. Be kind and
compassionate to one another, forgiving each other,
just as in Christ God forgave you.

—*Ephesians 4:31–32*

"Love means never having to say you're sorry."

Some of us who were around in the 1970s will remember
this line from the movie *Love Story*. Though it may have been
a hit movie, the line simply isn't true. Rather, living in a real
loving relationship will require the ability to not only say "I'm
sorry" but also to live in a posture of forgiveness, grace, and

restoration. Let's face it: we're all imperfect people who make mistakes. And since that's true, we need to learn the art of apologizing well.

Gary Chapman and Jennifer Thomas have written a very practical book that gives a simple outline for how to speak a language of apology more fluently. In *The Five Languages of Apology*, they explain what they call the five fundamental aspects or languages of an apology. Much like Chapman's classic *The 5 Love Languages*, the big idea of the book is that we each have a primary language of apology and we need to be aware of our own and our spouse's language. Here's the overview of the languages of apology:

- Expressing regret—"I am sorry."
- Accepting responsibility—"I was wrong."
- Making restitution—"What can I do to make it right?"
- Genuinely repenting—"I'll try not to do that again."
- Requesting forgiveness—"Will you please forgive me?"

Learning these languages of apology is certainly a good starting point for dealing with conflicts, disagreements, and hurts in our marriages. But there's more than just learning the right words to say. At the core, we must develop attitudes and hearts that are bent toward taking responsibility when we've wronged our spouse. That requires growth in humility. Let's face it: apologizing can really be difficult for some of us because we have to admit we're wrong. At times it's easier to justify and rationalize the behavior that was actually hurtful to our spouse.

Sometimes we offer a flippant "I'm sorry" in an effort to move on and not really own what's happened. A flippant apology is no apology at all. A good apology is always specific, offers no excuses or blame, and expresses regret and empathy. Additionally, a good apology offers more than words; it also takes action that shows that moving forward things will change and the offending behavior will not continue.

Ultimately, becoming a good apologizer is an important skill in growing intimacy in your marriage. The movie *Love Story* was wrong. The true statement is, "Love means often having to say you're sorry." And as we do that well, we will come to trust each other more, and unity grows in our marriage.

It takes one person to forgive; it takes two people to be reunited.

—Lewis B. Smedes, *The Art of Forgiving*

A MISSIONAL MARRIAGE

CHALLENGE 37

If you were given ten thousand dollars to invest in the life of someone else to encourage them, how would you spend it?

But be sure to fear the Lord and serve Him faithfully with all your heart; consider what great things He has done for you.

—*1 Samuel 12:24*

Several years ago I had the opportunity to spend a week in Haiti with a group of dads and their teenage children doing relief work, construction projects, and orphan care. While driving through the city of Port-au-Prince, it was overwhelming to think about all that needed to be accomplished in that city and country. Billions of dollars have been given to Haiti for relief efforts in the past few years, and yet the needs in that country remain great.

During our week in Haiti, one of the dads asked this question: "If you were given one hundred thousand dollars right now to invest in Haiti, what would you do that could help the maximum number of people?" As several of us dads discussed and dreamed about how we would use those dollars, we learned a lot about one another and how we viewed helping others. Our answers ranged from building schools to digging wells to food programs to microeconomic ventures. All of our answers were good and came from our dreaming. Since then, a couple of the dads have actually found a way to invest more in Haiti.

Today's question is similar. As you and your spouse spend time discussing how each of you would invest ten thousand dollars, listen to see what passions begin to surface. Listen to see how you think similarly and differently about encouraging and helping others. Remember, there's no one right or best way to offer help. As you listen to each other, be prepared to act. Although you may not have ten thousand dollars available to invest, you may discover a different way you can encourage and help someone. If so, take the risk and move in that direction. When we serve others *together*, it can provide a great avenue for intimacy and connection to grow.

It's easy for our marriages to become myopic and self-focused. Sometimes the greatest thing we can do for our marriages is to get outside of them and care for others. For some of us it can begin with a small step. We have some good friends who decided that the way they were going to serve others was through a weekly Sunday morning brunch with their unchurched neighbors. To do that, they had to start going to their church's Saturday night service so they were free on Sunday mornings. After doing that for several years, they would tell you it's been the best investment they've made in a long time—not just for their neighbors, but also for their marriage.

Going on mission together and caring for the needs of others has really strengthened them as a couple. And they did it without ten thousand dollars!

Marriage is foremost a vocation and a spiritual reality. A man and a woman come together for life to fulfill a mission that God has given them.

—Henri J. M. Nouwen,
Here and Now: Living in the Spirit

SIMPLE TRUTH

CHALLENGE 38

What are three simple phrases that describe
your desire for your marriage?

Be completely humble and gentle; be patient, bearing
with one another in love.

—*Ephesians 4:2*

College football season is the most wonderful time of year!
(Well, that seems to have nothing to do with intentionally
growing an intimate marriage, huh?) A couple of years ago,
some friends gave us tickets to take our two younger sons
to hear Tim Tebow, former quarterback of the University of
Florida Gators (there's the connection to college football!).
My boys were hypnotized as they listened to this college football legend speak about his faith and how he desires to live for

Christ daily. His words were a great encouragement for our sons.

Tebow's speech was composed of three simple phrases: be willing to stand alone, live with passion, and finish strong. He told stories of how he's had to take a stand to do what's right—even when the majority of people around him were choosing differently. He talked about the importance of living out of a deep passion—not merely going through the motions in life, but also living fully alive and not settling for the norm. And finally, he spoke about finishing strong—being determined never to quit no matter what the obstacles or challenges may be.

As I listened, I thought that his phrases could be great words for marriages in our culture.

Stand alone: go against the flow. Value the covenant of marriage. Acknowledge that God has a plan that's different from the conventional wisdom of our culture.

Live with passion: don't just survive marriage, thrive! Be committed to living out of awakened hearts and a deep passion toward God and your spouse.

Finish strong: look and plan for the long haul. It's trite but true: our marriages are not sprints, they are marathons.

As I thought about the 50 Fridays Marriage Challenge, I reflected upon the theme verse: "Teach us to number our days, that we may gain a heart of wisdom." Our marriages require a deep dependence on God's leading, a commitment to live in wisdom, and an intentionality to grow and change.

Few of us are ever going to be asked to speak to six thousand people at a local college. However, we could still benefit from developing our own simple three phrases that guide and encourage us on our journey toward intimacy in marriage. So what three phrases describe your desire for your marriage?

As God by creation made two of one, so again by marriage he made one of two.

—Thomas Adams, as quoted in *Gathered Gold*, edited by John Blanchard

IN THE BEGINNING

CHALLENGE 39

What are some of the most enjoyable memories, hobbies,
or habits from your first year of marriage?
Are those things that you still do?

Being confident of this, that He who began a good
work in you will carry it on to completion until the
day of Christ Jesus.

—*Philippians 1:6*

Often I hear couples reminiscing about the good ol' days. For
some couples, they are referring to the first few years of marriage. This is usually connected to a time without children
when there seemed to be more time to enjoy each other.
Sometimes the longing for the good ol' days is "code" for "we
don't do the things that we used to do anymore." Or maybe

what we really mean is, "*you* don't do the things that *you* used to do anymore!"

Life certainly has a way of getting busy. We are busy with so many good things for our work, our kids, our church, our schools, and our neighbors. These are really good! But with our busyness, we can let our marriage slip to the back burner. Things that used to be a priority can be forgotten, or we just stop doing them. Creative notes. Surprises. Flowers. Fun date nights. Stolen moments.

In Revelation 2, Jesus speaks to the church at Ephesus and affirms them for doing good deeds. But he says that they have one big problem: they have lost their first love. In the midst of doing so many things, they've forgotten how to really love their first love well. He could be talking about our marriages.

In verse 5, Jesus tells the church at Ephesus to do three things to restore their first love. Those three statements are good advice for our marriages as well.

First, *remember the heights from which you've fallen.* We need to take the time to remember where we used to be, what we used to enjoy, what we used to do together.

Second, *repent.* The word *repent* means to change directions—to stop going in one direction and to make a U-turn. Sometimes we need that type of radical change in our marriages. Sometimes it's just a small course correction.

Finally, *do the things you did at first.* I love this phrase! Maybe there's a place where you need to go back to the basics, enjoying the things you used to enjoy.

Those statements from Revelation 2 can be summarized with three short words: *Remember. Repent. Do.* Consider those words this week. Spend some time looking back. Then, wherever needed, change direction. And finally, do.

It's a good step in our growth toward authentic and intimate marriages!

Let the wife make her husband glad to come home and let him make her sorry to see him leave.

—Martin Luther, as quoted in
The Man in the Mirror, by Patrick Morley

40

TELLING STORIES

*What's a story from your marriage that you love to tell
or hear? What makes that story so special?*

One generation will commend your works to another;
they tell of your mighty acts. They speak of the glorious splendor of your majesty, and I will meditate on
your wonderful works.

—*Psalm 145:4–5*

My brother-in-law, Brian, is a great storyteller. When our
families are together, it's a very common occurrence for Brian
to have all of us leaning in to listen to one of his stories about
his past days of playing basketball or a recent event that has
happened or a challenge with a car. He has more car stories: a
car that caught on fire, a car that lost a wheel going down the

road, and a convertible that was crushed by a giant pumpkin! We've heard some of his stories a dozen times and yet never tire of hearing them.

At one of our Thanksgivings, twelve of us were gathered around the dining room table after our meal. We spent an hour or so as each person shared the things they were most thankful for from the past year. So many great stories: a fund started by my nephew to help a family in Kenya, a special father-son trip, the joy of a grandfather's recovery from a stroke, a testimony of a college freshman and God's faithfulness to him in a year of transition, a special time with family celebrating fifty years of marriage for my in-laws.

So many sweet stories. Stories that remind us of our roots. Stories that lead to worship. Stories that have an aroma of eternity. There's nothing like a good story. They make us laugh and remember and delight. But stories are more than that. As we tell stories, we remember. And it's in our remembering that we are often reminded of the faithfulness and the goodness and the provision of God. When the Old Testament Israelites forgot the stories of God, they moved toward idolatry and destruction. But in their remembering, their hearts turned toward surrender, confidence, and intimacy with their God.

The same is true in our remembering. Our remembering can lead us to an increase of faith, hope, and love—and any marriage can use more of those. So this week, take time to tell some stories. They may be about vacations, holidays, car challenges, the birth of children, moments of loss, a time of redemption, surprise parties, or special gifts. Whatever the stories, they are a great way for us to connect and enjoy the days we've shared and to anticipate the making of more stories in the days ahead.

A story is based on what people think is important, so when we live a story, we are telling people around us what we think is important.

—Donald Miller, *A Million Miles in a Thousand Years*

41

THE POWER OF
THE TONGUE

CHALLENGE 41
*How do you use your words in
the midst of conflict in your marriage?*

The tongue has the power of life and death, and those
who love it will eat its fruit.

—*Proverbs 18:21*

What does it mean when a traffic light turns yellow? Unfortunately, for many of us it means hurry up and get through the light! We know that a yellow light is supposed to encourage us to slow down and be prepared to stop. Blowing through a yellow light is dangerous and can lead to tragedy. At times we do the same thing in our relationship: we ignore some yellow lights during our communication and instead of preparing to stop before we continue, we speed up and end up in difficult situations where we choose our words poorly and do damage to our marriage. There is great wisdom in pausing and thinking about what we're going to say. It's why James encourages us to be slow to speak and quick to listen. Sometimes we need to sit at a red light for several seconds before we proceed with a green light.

In Ephesians 4:25–32, Paul gives us four red light/green light guidelines that help us use our words well in times of conflict. He is writing and giving some very practical advice on things we need to put off (red light) and other things we need to add (green light) to how we relate to each other. Find some time this week to grab your Bibles and look at these few verses together as a framework for better communication during conflict. These are really practical ways of watching our words. Here's an overview of what you'll see:

Verse	Principle	Red Light	Green Light
Ephesians 4:25	Always tell the truth.	Stop lying.	Speak truthfully.
Ephesians 4:26–27	Own your anger; don't let your anger own you.	Don't sin in your anger.	Deal with your anger well.
Ephesians 4:29–30	Your words really matter— watch them carefully.	Put off unwholesome talk.	Speak words of life that build up and encourage.

Ephesians 4:31–32	Your posture and emotional attitude are as important as your words.	Lay aside a malicious attitude.	Embrace compassion, kindness, and forgiveness.

After you've spent some time reading this passage together, take the next step and share with each other which of these guidelines are most applicable to you. Which of these principles do you often violate and run the red light? What could you do differently when you realize that you're about to run through a yellow light? Do you need to apologize to your spouse regarding a recent conflict or a habit that's been created?

Remember Solomon's words from our verse for today: "The tongue has the power of life and death." We can avoid some accidents by paying more attention to how we use our words.

> The amount of conflict in a marriage only determines the speed at which the marriage is moving toward greatness or destruction.
>
> —Neil Clark Warren, *The Triumphant Marriage*

42

I'M SCARED!

CHALLENGE 42

What things scare you? When you look ahead to the next few months, what things are you afraid of or concerned about?

So do not fear, for I am with you; do not be dismayed,
for I am your God. I will strengthen you and help you;
I will uphold you with my righteous right hand.

—*Isaiah 41:10*

Recently I read an article that discussed the different fears that many of us have.

According to one website, there are more than 530 different phobias! Here are some of the common ones:

- Arachnophobia—fear of spiders
- Claustrophobia—fear of being trapped in small spaces

- Acrophobia—fear of heights
- Atychiphobia—fear of failure

I found a few fun ones too:

- Ephebiphobia—fear of teenagers
- Dentophobia—fear of dentists
- Elurophobia—fear of cats (not to be confused with hatred of cats!)
- Phobophobia—fear of phobias

We may or may not identify with any of these phobias, but for all of us, fear is a real part of life. When we embrace fear in a healthy way, it becomes a warning light that tells us we need to trust God's goodness and faithfulness in the midst of a specific situation. When we ignore our fear, it can paralyze us or lead us toward destructive behavior. In our marriages, un-recognized fear often leads us to destructive behavior. On the one hand, fear can cause us to shut down and be filled with anxiety. In those times we use words such as "overwhelmed" and "concerned" when really we may be unaware of our fear. In other situations, being unaware of our fear can cause us to escalate and try to control everything and everyone around us. When that happens, we can rage and attack others as we try to gain a sense of control or reestablish what we think is right and good.

Fear is a topic that the Bible is quick to address and does

so frequently. As you may know, the command "fear not" is the most common command in the Bible. Some commentators say that "fear not" appears 366 times in the Bible—one for every day of the year, including a leap year. Many times that command is linked with a phrase such as "for I am with you." In other words, along with the command to "not fear," God offers us the promise and comfort of His presence in every situation. God knew that fear would be real in this broken world, and so He regularly reminds us that He is enough when our fear rises.

As you answer this week's question, spend time together reading out loud the following passages: Isaiah 43:1–2, Isaiah 41:10, Deuteronomy 31:8, Joshua 1:9, 1 Peter 5:7. Let God's Word guide you in a time of prayer to surrender your fears to Him and to celebrate the truth that His presence is with you in every situation.

> Thinking runaway, worrisome thoughts is just an invitation to anxiety.
>
> —Lisa TerKeurst, *Unglued*

43

LOVING CHRIST

CHALLENGE 43

Describe your love life with Christ.
How do you grow in your intimacy with Him?

By wisdom a house is built, and through understanding it is established; through knowledge its rooms are
filled with rare and beautiful treasures.

—Proverbs 24:3–4

Think of a triangle.

Many of us have seen a triangle used to represent how our
marriages grow—especially in the area of spiritual intimacy.
God is at the top, and you and your spouse are at opposite
ends on the bottom of the triangle. As each of you moves
closer to Christ, you are also growing closer to each other.

As believers, we know that our ability to love comes from

the reality that we've first been loved by God. His initiation toward us empowers us to respond in love. The first and primary object worthy of that response is God. In His kindness, He has set up marriage in such a way that when each of us lives into our love relationship with Him, our marriage can grow in intimacy as well.

So often we try to grow intimacy in our marriages along the bottom line of the triangle only. We work harder. We communicate better. We have more dates. We share with others. We spend more time together. All of these things are good practices, but the first movement to grow intimacy in our marriage is upward!

There are a number of ways by which we can move toward Christ individually. At the center of our spiritual growth are the habits of praying and time in the Bible. Developing those habits—or spiritual disciplines—individually is the starting point of how we grow in our walk with Christ. If this is something that's not a regular part of your life currently, make a commitment to spend ten to fifteen minutes a day praying and reading a short passage of Scripture for a month. One easy way to do that is to read one proverb each day. There are thirty-one proverbs, so you can read the proverb that corresponds with whatever day is on the calendar.

This week, look for ways to encourage your spouse in his or her love relationship with Christ. As you both diligently and passionately pursue Him, watch what happens between the two of you! Make time regularly to share with each other what you are reading or learning and pondering. Some of the best conversations come as we share with each other how we're experiencing God's love and guidance in our lives. But be prepared: pursuing Christ passionately will always invite us to travel a road marked with surrender, repentance, forgiveness, and obedience. As God's truth grows in us, it may challenge and convict us to change and deal with some things we've been ignoring. And that is a road worth traveling!

When I have learnt to love God better than my earthly dearest, I shall love my earthly dearest better than I do now.

—C. S. Lewis, *The Collected Letters of C. S. Lewis*

LIONS, TIGERS, AND BEARS, OH, MY!

In the midst of conflict, what animal are you most like?

A gentle answer turns away wrath, but a harsh word stirs up anger. The tongue of the wise commends knowledge, but the mouth of the fool gushes folly.

—*Proverbs 15:1–2*

Conflict in marriage is inevitable. And yet conflict is never the problem in a marriage; rather, the inability to resolve conflicts in a healthy manner is what can cause damage and even destruction in our marriages. One of the barriers that keep us from resolving conflict well is having a negative style in the midst of conflict. An easy way to identify our styles of conflict resolution is by comparing them to different animals.

Turtle. Some of us have a turtle-like style to conflict resolution, and we avoid conflict at all cost. When things become difficult or tense in our marriage, we retreat into our shells. When this happens, communication comes to an abrupt halt.

Teddy bear. Others of us become a sweet and cuddly teddy bear and accommodate our spouse's ideas, views, or desires without ever stopping to consider what we really want or need in the midst of conflict.

Fox. Most of have heard the phrase "sly as a fox" and know that it creates the image of people who are cunning and even manipulative to get their way. This style leaves one person winning and one person losing.

Shark. For some, conflict brings out the attacking side of our personality. Sharks can smell blood in the water during conflict, and they can suddenly attack. Unfortunately, sharks often attack the person instead of the issue and create a win-lose situation.

Hyena. In the Disney classic *The Lion King*, the hyenas were the comic relief characters. In conflict resolution, a hyena learns to make a joke in any situation and can use humor to hide from difficult issues.

We obviously could think of other animals that represent a negative style of conflict resolution (scared like a chicken, burying your head in the sand like an ostrich, flying away like an eagle, stubborn as a mule). All of these styles represent negative ways of engaging in conflict by either exclusively focusing on our wants, avoiding the situation, or giving in to our spouse and ignoring our wants. That's where another animal comes in that models good conflict resolution skills: the *owl*.

For years, the owl has been a symbol of wisdom in many cultures. To engage in conflict in a healthy and profitable style requires wisdom that is rooted in collaboration. When we approach conflict with a collaborative style, we value our spouses and make sure our voices and wants are being spoken. When both husband and wife approach conflict in a collaborative fashion, great conflict resolution can be the result.

So in marriage, genuine peace does not mean the absence of all conflict. It means that when conflicts arise, they are handled and resolved biblically because loving, pleasing, and honoring God is reestablished as our greatest desire and pursuit.

—Gary and Betsy Ricucci, *Love That Lasts*

45

COUNT YOUR BLESSINGS

CHALLENGE 45
*What are ten blessings that you
have received in the past month?*

Every good and perfect gift is from above, coming
down from the Father of the heavenly lights, who
does not change like shifting shadows.

—*James 1:17*

I heard bestselling author and business thinker Jim Collins address a large group of leaders on the topic of his book *How the Mighty Fall*. In this book, Collins shares his research on why seemingly great companies struggle, decline, and eventually fail. His premise is pretty simple: decline can be avoided, detected, and reversed. In other words, destruction doesn't have to be the end; there is hope for change in an organization.

Toward the end of his talk, he shared some steps for organizations to take when they recognize difficult times. His second step was "Count Your Blessings." His point was simple: as you begin to account for all the good things that have happened to you—things you did not cause—it's a very humbling and encouraging experience.

I'd take it one step further. When we count our blessings, it can lead us to worship, praise, and express gratitude to the One who is the Giver of Blessings. And that's a good exercise to experience regularly in our marriages. In our busy lives, it's easy to get focused on what's not happening or to ponder the challenges ahead or to become paralyzed by the tyranny of today's agenda.

There are certain times when we can't see the blessings that are all around us. Making a list of ten blessings in the past thirty days might be a difficult exercise for you. But I'm certain of this: there are at least ten blessings we've all received in the past thirty days. When we stop and consider the ways we have been blessed—regardless of our current situation—it's always good for us. Throughout the Psalms, we often read of how difficult or trying something may be, but frequently the psalmist's response is to give thanks for the provision, goodness, and blessing of God.

As we count our blessings, our hearts can grow in gratitude. And people with grateful hearts make wonderful spouses! By the way, for those of us who are parents, counting your blessings is a great family exercise. Here's a thought: after dinner one night give everyone a piece of paper and have them make a list of their top ten blessings and then share with one another. Those pieces of paper would make great "wallpaper" for the fridge.

There are only two ways to live your life. One is as though nothing is a miracle. The other is as though everything is a miracle.

—Albert Einstein, *The Ultimate Quotable Einstein*

CREATING A SAFE PLACE

CHALLENGE 46
How would you evaluate your spouse's listening skills?
How about your skills? What are some of
your barriers to listening well?

He who answers before listening—that is his folly and his shame.

—*Proverbs 18:13*

When my dad purchased hearing aids, he became a changed man. While walking out of the doctor's office after getting them, he took a few steps and then stopped and asked, "What is that noise?" Not hearing it, he would start back walking and after a few steps he stopped again and said, "There it is again. Do you hear it?" After several repeat occurrences of this mystery noise, I realized that with every step my dad was taking he was hearing his shoes on the sidewalk! Yes, he really was that deaf.

Most of us are blessed with the ability to hear, but hearing and listening are two different things. Listening well implies not only hearing words but also seeking to understand them. And that requires a commitment to the hard work of listening. Next week we will look at some practical ways to improve your listening skills. For today, let's take a quick look at some common barriers that prevent us from really hearing what our spouse is saying.

Rebuttal listening. Rebuttal listening comes in many shapes and sizes. One of the most common forms is when you partially listen but spend most of your energy preparing your response or rebuttal to what you've heard. The energy is focused on your response instead of on your spouse's message.

Fix-it listening. Men, this can often be a big listening barrier style for us. We hear something, and we immediately offer advice to fix it. After all, every problem has a solution, right?

Half listening. Some of us can be guilty of not really listening, but nodding regularly and saying "yes, dear" at the right time. When this happens, we hear words but don't really take in the message. This barrier can be caused by distractions, apathy, or fatigue at the end of a long day.

Mind reading. Another barrier to listening is when we try to mind read. Mind reading happens especially when our spouse is talking about a familiar topic and we assume we know what he or she thinks and feels. Mind reading can be dismissive and hurtful.

Avoiding. In some situations, couples develop a barrier to listening by avoiding conversations that need to take place. At other times, the conversation begins, and then one spouse withdraws or walks away. Obviously, when we avoid or withdraw, healthy listening cannot occur.

Interrupting. Maybe one of the most common barriers to listening well is interrupting. When both husband and wife are talking at the same time, there is no possibility of healthy communication.

There are many barriers to being able to really listen well. These are just a few. Which one of these (or maybe a different barrier) prevents you from communicating in the best way possible in your marriage?

The first duty of love is to listen.

—Paul Tillich, as quoted in
The Friendship Factor,
by Alan Loy McGinnis

47

LISTENING COURAGEOUSLY

CHALLENGE 47
How can you improve your listening skills?

My dear brothers and sisters, take note of this: Everyone should be quick to listen, slow to speak, and slow to become angry.

—*James 1:19*

Developing good listening skills is critical for an intimate and healthy marriage. One technique that helps minimize negative listening patterns is the "speaker-listener technique." It's as simple as it sounds: in communication, one of us is the speaker and one of us is the listener. Slowing down our conversations often provides the space for understanding, empathy, and clarity. This skill is certainly not necessary in every conversation;

however, when communication gets difficult or bogged down, this technique can be a real help. Although it's discussed in many marriage and communication books, the book *Fighting for Your Marriage*, by Howard Markman, Scott Stanley, and Susan Blumberg, has developed eight simple rules that help make this technique work well.

Rules for both the speaker and the listener

1. *The speaker has the floor.* Only one speaker per conversation. The other person is the listener.
2. *Share the floor.* Over the course of the conversation, the speaker and listener will switch roles.
3. *No problem solving.* The focus is good discussion, not solutions.

Rules for the speaker

1. *Speak for yourself.* Don't try to be a mind reader. Use "I" statements ("I think you're crazy!" is not an "I" statement). Talk about *your* feelings, thoughts, and concerns.
2. *Don't go on and on.* There is plenty of opportunity to add more. Try to help the listener by speaking in manageable statements.
3. *Stop and let the listener paraphrase.* After you've spoken, stop and allow the listener time to paraphrase

what you've said. If understanding has happened, continue. If not, restate.

Rules for the listener

1. *Paraphrase what you hear.* Briefly repeat what you heard using your own words. Show that you were listening.
2. *Focus on the speaker's message.* Don't rebut. Don't offer your opinion or your thoughts when you are the listener. You are only trying to understand what has been spoken.

When first using this technique, it seems very mechanical and artificial. I often compare it to having a cast on a broken leg. The cast restricts your movement, makes you walk differently, slows your pace, and feels awkward. However, that same cast is providing an environment for healing of the broken bone; and once healed, the bone is stronger. In similar fashion, using the speaker-listener technique can create a safe environment for us to communicate clearly and experience a better way of relating and connecting as we learn to really listen to our spouse.

Courage is what it takes to stand up and speak; courage is also what it takes to sit down and listen.

—Winston Churchill, *Churchill by Himself*

THE HEART OF
THE MATTER

CHALLENGE 48

What are three things that happened this past week?
How did you feel about them?

Out of the abundance of the heart, the mouth speaks.
—*Matthew 12:34, ESV*

One of the biggest challenges of maturity is coming to understand how our actions and our heart connect with each other. Many people never understand the world of feelings and emotions, and they end up stunted in their growth and development. We tend to stay in the rational side of life, where we try to think everything through and understand it cognitively only. People often do one of two things with feelings: they either make them the most important thing in the world *or* they completely ignore them, as if they don't exist. Neither way works very well.

All of us have feelings. Some scientists believe that we have feelings before we even have thoughts. To really understand what's going on in life, you must learn to name what you are feeling. Honestly, over time this needs to become second nature—to know what you are feeling, not just what you are thinking. Sometimes you can't get to what you really think and believe until you deal with what you're feeling.

The problem is that we create a list of feelings that's a mile long. I've seen them with as many as fifty different feelings or emotions listed. People who really study the world of feelings tell us that there's only a handful of emotions—between three and nine in most books. Some books will often differentiate between "good" emotions and "bad" emotions. So here's a quick test for you: Which of these feelings are the good ones—hurt, sad, lonely, surprise, fear, anger, guilt, shame, joy?

When most people look at this list, they'll say that joy is the only good one. The truth is that all nine of these feelings can have a huge benefit as well as a big dark side. For example, anger or fear can motivate you toward hurting someone or it can motivate you to save someone. The emotion itself is not the problem. What we do with it, however, is very important.

One of the exercises we've learned over the past few years is to have an emotional check-in from time to time. An emotional check-in is as simple as taking a few minutes and asking these questions: "In light of what's been going on today, what have you been feeling? What are you feeling right now?" For several years we had a list of eight emotions that hung on our refrigerator door. This list became the "cheat sheet" when we needed to describe what we were feeling. Over time we have developed a language that allows us to better understand what we are feeling. As we slow down and realize what's going on inside of us, it opens opportunities for us to connect at a deeper level and to understand each other more fully.

God made us emotional and rational beings. The two go hand in hand. They support, define, and clarify each other. Emotion and reason together are what make us complete and make our lives full.

—Matthew Elliott, *Feel: The Power of Listening to Your Heart*

49

ARE YOU SAFE?

CHALLENGE 49

*What's one thing your spouse does that makes you
feel safe in sharing your thoughts and feelings?*

Dear friends, let us love one another, for love comes
from God. Everyone who loves has been born of God
and knows God. Whoever does not love does not
know God, because God is love.

—*1 John 4:7–8*

Over the past couple of decades, much research has been
conducted in the area of the science of love in order to learn
how we love and connect. One of the strongest voices in that
field is Dr. Sue Johnson, who has written a book titled *Hold
Me Tight.* Johnson's basic idea in her research and book is that
our marriages require a safe emotional connection to experience intimacy and love. Safety grows as we come to trust our

partner's ability and availability to be present. In other words, if we're really going to connect intimately with each other, we need to know that we're safe with each other.

When we feel safe, we can more freely and deeply attach to and connect with our spouse. But what does "feeling safe" really mean? At the core of who we are, Johnson says, all of us ask this basic question about our spouse: "Are you going to be there for me?" In her book she uses the acronym ARE to address the three basic needs for creating a safe environment together: accessibility, responsiveness, and engagement. Johnson offers couples three simple questions that further explain those words and how they help grow a safe emotional connection. By answering these questions about yourself and your spouse, you can continue to grow in your availability to your spouse.

First, are you *accessible* when I try to reach out to you? Healthy emotional connection begins with accessibility, and that obviously requires time spent together. I can be in the same room with Lora and be miles away—especially during college football season! When one spouse asks the other for a few minutes to talk, making yourself accessible is critical to good conversation and connection. Developing simple habits of prioritizing time without interruptions and making eye contact during communication are important steps in being available and accessible to our spouse.

Second, will you be *responsive* to my needs? When a spouse asks for something they need, that is a very vulnerable position. Strong emotional connection happens when we learn to be responsive to those moments. For years I thought I had to say "yes" to a need in order to be responsive. However, when children came along, I quickly realized that responsiveness is not connected to a "yes" or a "no"; rather, it's a posture of connection that may best be defined as curiosity. A responsive spouse is one who works hard to understand, hear, and act on their spouse's requests.

Third, are you *engaged* in this relationship? It is possible to be accessible and responsive and not be really engaged. It's what we call "going through the motions." Some of us have learned to use the "yes, dear" and "oh, sure, honey" responses that can mimic accessibility and responsiveness. However, really being engaged prioritizes our marriage and says, "I'm invested, I'm committed, I'm present." When we are engaged with each other, our confidence in our relationship grows and we can take risks for deeper intimacy.

Three simple words: *accessibility*, *responsiveness*, and *engagement*. Together, they are the building blocks for creating and growing the foundation for a safe and emotionally connected marriage.

Intimacy can grow only in a place of safety. When husband and wife are afraid of hurt, rebuff, criticism, and misunderstanding, they will find it difficult to touch and share freely. . . . If you want real intimacy in your marriage, you will have to establish trust in your relationship.

—Ed Wheat, *Love Life for Every Married Couple*

50

THE MOST INTIMATE ACT

CHALLENGE 50

How often do you pray out loud with each other?
What changes (if any) would you like to see in that area?

Again, I tell you that if two of you on earth agree
about anything you ask for, it will be done for you by
my Father in heaven. For where two or three come
together in my name, there am I with them.

—Matthew 18:19–20

For the first several years of our marriage, I would have an-
swered today's questions by saying that we pray together daily,
and almost all of that was prayer before dinner! Taking a moment and giving thanks for God's provision before a meal is
a fine discipline to develop and I'm glad we did. But there's
another level of prayer that we often found to be very difficult
in our marriage.

Over the years, I've discovered that many couples struggle in the area of praying together, and they often wonder why this is so hard to do. Although many married people would say that they regularly pray *for* their spouse, praying *with* each other is often a great challenge. And yet sociologist Andrew Greeley surveyed married couples and found that the happiest couples were those who prayed *together!*

Authors Les and Leslie Parrott explain it this way in their book *Saving Your Marriage Before It Starts*: "Couples who frequently pray together are twice as likely as those who pray less often to describe their marriages as being highly romantic. And get this—married couples who pray together are 90 percent more likely to report higher satisfaction with their sex lives. Prayer, because of the vulnerability it demands, also draws a couple closer."

The most intimate act we can enjoy together is praying together. In prayer, our hearts can be moved toward intimacy with our Father and deeper intimacy with each other. If this is an area where your marriage can grow, start small. Find a time this week to pray together with each other, even if just for a few minutes.

This doesn't need to become legalistic for you. You will not find a command anywhere in the Bible that says a husband and wife should pray with each other every day. Some of us were raised in traditions where praying out loud or with someone else was not common, and therefore, doing so can be intimidating or difficult. Sometimes using a prayer book and reading written prayers together is a good starting point.

When we think of prayer as a simple conversation with the God we both call Father, it can help us take the risk to pray with each other by simply having a conversation with Him together. There's no right or wrong way to do this, but it's certainly a challenge that can help develop a deeper level of spiritual intimacy.

Nothing tends more to cement the hearts of Christians than praying together. Never do they love one another so well as when they witness the outpouring of each other's hearts in prayer.

—Charles G. Finney, *Lectures on Revivals of Religion*

EPILOGUE

"For I know the plans I have for you," declares the
LORD, "plans to prosper you and not to harm you,
plans to give you hope and a future."

—*Jeremiah 29:11*

Well, we have come to the end of the 50 Fridays Marriage
Challenge. If you've made it this far, well done! We hope
these weekly questions have encouraged deeper conversation
and connection for you in your marriage. Developing the
discipline to check in with each other weekly is a great foun-
dational building block for growing a healthy and intimate
marriage. At the core, we hope you've grown in authenticity,
transparency, and vulnerability with each other.

So here's a last question for the 50 Fridays Marriage Challenge . . . actually two challenges for you today:

First: Every year in December, there are a number of "Best of" lists as we look back on the year. These lists range from music hits to movies to sports moments. I love looking back at the best catches of the year or the best come-from-behind victories. Highlight videos are always a blast to watch. In a similar fashion, it's fun to develop your own "Best of" list—call it the "Best of Our Marriage Highlights." As you look back on the past year of the 50 Fridays Marriage Challenge, what have been some of the highlights in your marriage? To help you with your highlights, think of these areas:

- Vacation
- Spiritual growth
- Transitions (moves, job, graduation, etc.)
- Communication and conflict resolution
- Hobbies
- Financial- or budget-related
- Date nights
- Time with friends
- Serving others

Second: What goals can you set for the next year of your life together? Use the highlights list above to help you set a goal (or two) for your marriage for this next year. At the beginning of this book, we read the words from Moses in Psalm 90:12: "Teach us to number our days aright, that we may gain a heart of wisdom." Part of numbering our days aright requires us to be intentional in how we connect and how we love. Having some goals or dreams for the next season of life helps us be intentional in moving forward in our intimacy and connection.

We all know the importance of this. Marriage is under fire in our culture. Most of us have watched marriages that seemed strong and healthy deteriorate and end in divorce. All around us we are reminded of the low value of marriage and commitment. We are bombarded with images of failure and pain in marriages. As we're writing this, national headlines scream out about the divorce rate, major government leaders and their infidelity scandals, and domestic violence in the homes of world-class athletes.

One of the myths of marriages is that marriage is supposed to be easy. We're not sure where that idea comes from, but it's certainly a myth. Growing an intimate marriage doesn't just happen. It requires intentionality. It requires commitment. It requires work. And it requires time. That all adds up to perseverance. The sports world is filled with quotes, slogans, and cheers about not quitting or giving up. Athletes are encouraged to "finish strong," "not quit," "push through the pain," and "fight to the finish."

Our marriages are worth fighting for, but both of us must be committed to the same value and desire. In 1993, Lora and I joined a small group through our church while living near Chicago. Shortly after we joined them, one of the people in the group challenged all of us to have "countercultural marriages." He went on to explain his terminology. He said that if we have a cultural marriage, two or three of our marriages should end in divorce within the next couple of years, and then he looked around the room and asked which couples it would be! It was through that group that we reaffirmed our desire to be intentional in growing our marriage.

And that's the message we hope you'll continue to embrace: your marriage is worth the effort. Intentionally growing intimacy honors God and leaves a legacy for those behind us to follow. It's never a question of "Will we leave a legacy?" The real question is "What kind of legacy will we leave?" When we arrive at our golden wedding anniversary and we're celebrating fifty years together, may others look at us and be amazed at what God has done in us and through us. And most important, may our children and those closest to us look at us and know that what others see is the truth of how we've lived and how we've loved.

> To love at all is to be vulnerable. Love anything and your heart will be wrung and possibly broken. If you want to make sure of keeping it intact you must give it to no one, not even an animal. Wrap it carefully round with hobbies and little luxuries; avoid all entanglements. Lock it up safe in the casket or coffin of your selfishness. But in that casket, safe, dark, motionless, airless, it will change. It will not be broken; it will become unbreakable, impenetrable, irredeemable. To love is to be vulnerable.
>
> —C. S. Lewis, *The Four Loves*

Bonus Section

FOR HOLIDAYS AND SPECIAL DAYS

VALENTINE'S DAY

CHALLENGE
What would you like to do on Valentine's Day?

There is no fear in love. But perfect love drives out fear, because fear has to do with punishment. The one who fears is not made perfect in love. We love because He first loved us.

—*1 John 4:18–19*

When I was in elementary school, one of the most stressful days of the year was Valentine's Day. For several days leading up to February 14, all of us made our personalized mailbox—using materials such as a cereal box, oatmeal canister, or shoe box with tons of glitter, construction paper, and paint.

Then the dreaded day came. I brought in my mailbox and waited to see if anyone would give me a Valentine's card.

I didn't understand at the time that every child *had* to bring enough cards for everyone in the class! When the day was over and I realized that my mailbox was filled with Valentine's cards, I couldn't wait to get home and read them. Actually, I just looked through the cards and found the ones that had small candy bars taped to them!

Years have passed, and my stress about Valentine's Day is gone. Even though this day is just another "Hallmark holiday" rooted in no meaningful history, I've learned to enjoy it. For all of our marriages, it's good to have a day that encourages intentionality and creativity in expressing our love to each other. It may come through flowers, cards, balloons, special dates, long walks, a romantic evening, or candy! You may go out to a fun restaurant, cook together at home, or order in. You may watch a movie or go to a symphony.

One important thing to do before Valentine's Day is to ask today's question of each other. It's an easy way to make sure you know each other's expectations and can help you enjoy this day together. Actually, that's a great way to live every day of the year—not just on this Hallmark holiday.

So, in the middle of these winter days, warm up your love life on this Valentine's Day. Take some time to talk, make a fun plan, express your love creatively to your spouse, and enjoy the love of your life. And remember, as our verse reminds us today, the reason we can love each other well is because we have first been loved by our heavenly Father. His love empowers us to move beyond our fear and to engage passionately.

If we are to develop an intimate relationship, we need to know each other's desires. If we wish to love each other, we need to know what the other person wants.

—Gary Chapman, *The 5 Love Languages*

PALM SUNDAY

CHALLENGE

How can you intentionally remember and reflect upon
Jesus during this upcoming Holy Week?

They took palm branches and went out to meet Him,
shouting, "Hosanna!" "Blessed is he who comes in the
name of the LORD!" "Blessed is the King of Israel!"

—*John 12:13*

Often, we rush to Easter and miss the importance of the week
leading up to that glorious morning. The Sunday before Easter
is Palm Sunday, when we begin Holy Week or Passion Week—
the last week in the life of Jesus. Over the years I've developed
a tradition of intentionally reading and reflecting on the life of
Jesus during this week. I start on Palm Sunday as I imagine the
cheers and praises of the triumphal entry to Jerusalem. I follow

the events of that week by reading the different gospel writers' accounts (as best as possible) that culminate with the suffering, crucifixion, death, and burial of Jesus.

In addition to reading the biblical passages, I usually read a book about the cross. Some of my favorites are:

The Cross of Christ, by John R. W. Stott

Fifty Reasons Why Jesus Came to Die, by John Piper

The Case for Christ, by Lee Strobel

Contemplating the Cross, by Tricia Rhodes

A Violent Grace, by Michael Card

Reliving the Passion, by Walter Wangerin, Jr.

Six Hours One Friday, by Max Lucado

In My Place Condemned He Stood, by J. I. Packer and
   Mark Dever

I started this tradition in 1992—the year after my younger brother died unexpectedly during the Easter season of 1991. It's always been a beneficial tradition for me. As I reflect more on the work of Christ, it increases my gratitude and worship on Easter Sunday. It also reminds me of the eternal hope that Easter provides.

What could you do together this week to help you intentionally remember and reflect upon the gracious gift of Jesus? Maybe it's as simple as reading Isaiah 53 together. Or perhaps you can watch the movie *The Passion of the Christ*.

I encourage you to take the time this week to think about

the greatest love gift ever given to us—God giving His Son. All that we long for in our marriages must first be found in His selfless, scandalous, sacrificial cross.

God beckons us to gaze in awe at what we see at Calvary's mount. He challenges us to bathe in the wonder of such love until we lay ourselves down weary with unworthiness, yet cleansed and renewed in the healing stream of blood shed there.

—Tricia Rhodes, *Contemplating the Cross*

GOOD FRIDAY AND EASTER

CHALLENGE

What do Good Friday and Easter mean to you?

Jesus said to her, "I am the resurrection and the life. He who believes in me will live, even though he dies; and whoever lives and believes in me will never die. Do you believe this?"

—*John 11:25–26*

Many years ago I heard Tony Campolo tell the story of his pastor preaching a Good Friday sermon and primarily using the phrase "It's Friday, but Sunday's coming." Campolo tells the story like this:

He [an older African American pastor] started his sermon real softly by saying, "It was Friday; and my Jesus was dead on the tree. But that was Friday, and Sunday's coming!" One of the deacons yelled, "Preach, brother, preach!" It was all the encouragement he needed. He came on louder as he said, "It was Friday, and Mary was crying her eyes out. The disciples were running in every direction, like sheep without a shepherd, but that was Friday, and Sunday's coming!"

The preacher kept going. He picked up the volume still more and shouted, "It was Friday. The cynics were looking at the world and saying, 'As things have been so shall they be. You can't change anything in this world; you can't change anything.' But those cynics don't know that it was only Friday. Sunday's coming! It was Friday, and Pilate thought he had washed his hands of a lot of trouble. The Pharisees were strutting around, laughing and poking each other in the ribs. They thought they were back in charge of things. But they didn't know it was only Friday! Sunday's coming!"

He kept on working that one phrase for a half hour, then an hour, then an hour and a quarter, then an hour and a half. Over and over he came at us, "It's Friday, but Sunday's coming!" By the time he had come to the end of the message . . . he had me and everybody else so worked up that I don't think any of us could have stood it much longer. At the end of his message he just yelled at the top of his lungs, "It's

FRIDAY!" and all five hundred of us in that church yelled back with one accord, "SUNDAY'S COMING!"

We all know the feeling of our own "Fridays" when life seems not to work, when dreams die, when things don't make sense, when hope seems distant. This day in history—Good Friday—reminds all of us that there is more going on than what we see. On that first Good Friday, the disciples had lost all hope. Their dreams had been shattered. Their life was placed into a borrowed tomb.

But that was Friday. Sunday's coming.

What a difference the next few hours made! The exclamation point of Easter Sunday proclaims that new life is always available, redemption is possible, hope is near, death is not the last word, God is good.

Take time as a couple this Easter weekend to remember and consider and worship the One who has changed everything forever and ever. Amen.

It's Friday. But Sunday's coming!

God proved His love on the Cross. When Christ hung, and bled, and died, it was God saying to the world, "I love you."

—Billy Graham

THANKSGIVING

CHALLENGE

Where do you see God's faithfulness and mercy in your life and marriage? What things are you thankful for this season?

The steadfast love of the LORD never ceases;
His mercies never come to an end;
they are new every morning;
great is your faithfulness.

—Lamentations 3:22–23 (ESV)

Every Thanksgiving season, I find myself reflecting on the words of the old hymn "Great Is Thy Faithfulness," which was inspired by the passage above. Thanksgiving provides a natural opportunity for us to pause and remember God's steadfast love, unceasing mercies, and great faithfulness. As we consider

His great faithfulness, we naturally respond with gratitude, praise, and thanksgiving.

Or do we?

Grab your Bible, turn to Luke 17:11–19, and read the story of Jesus healing the ten lepers. In our busy lives, it's easy to be like "the nine" who enjoyed God's blessing of healing but didn't stop to say "thank you." It's equally easy to do that in our marriages and with our spouses. We enjoy all that we get, yet at times we don't stop to say thanks. Learning to slow down and express gratitude is a daily discipline worth developing in our marriages.

Thanksgiving is a natural time to work on this. For years we've had a simple family Thanksgiving tradition of having everyone at the table share a few things they are thankful for as they reflect on the previous year. Sometimes it goes quickly. Other years, we stop and tell lengthy stories to remind one another of God's goodness and to rejoice in His provision. There's something about gratitude that draws you together.

Take advantage of this upcoming holiday to be intentional in expressing your gratitude to your spouse, to those you love, and to the One who loved you so much that He chose to die rather than live without you.

Enjoy your Thanksgiving!

If the only prayer you said in your whole life was "Thank you," that would suffice.

—Meister Eckhart, fourteenth-century German theologian

MERRY CHRISTMAS!

CHALLENGE

What's your favorite memory from Christmas as a child?
What's your favorite memory from Christmas
since you've been married?

So they hurried off and found Mary and Joseph, and the baby, who was lying in the manger. When they had seen him, they spread the word concerning what had been told them about this child, and all who heard it were amazed at what the shepherds said to them. But Mary treasured up all these things and pondered them in her heart.

—Luke 2:16–19

Mary's story always amazes me. While a young teenage girl, an angel appears to her and tells her that she's going to have a baby—even though she's never been with a man! Instead of laughing or thinking she's crazy or running away, she responds with a gentle spirit of obedience. God provides Joseph, as a man of amazing faith, to walk with her and to become her husband. And together these two end up in Bethlehem and participate in the birth of the Christ child.

There's a lot of excitement and action around those early days and years of Jesus' life. Visits from shepherds and kings—the lowly and the highest. Imagine the conversations that she must have heard! Toward the end of Luke's account of Jesus' birth in Luke 2:19, this little phrase shows up: "But Mary treasured up all these things and pondered them in her heart." Sometimes, when we've seen and heard amazing things, the best thing we can do is to treasure those moments in our hearts.

Christmas is the time of year when many special moments can happen. Most of us have some "treasures" from past Christmases stored up in our hearts. When we slow down and remember those stories, they are great to share with each other. Sometimes those memories are connected to special gifts or to serving or to people. As we remember those treasures, we open up a special part of our hearts to each other.

One of the stories that I carry in my heart is connected to the Christmas after my mom died. I was twenty years old when my mom died in late November. That Christmas was entirely different than the previous two decades had been. My father, younger brother, and I didn't decorate the house. There was no Christmas music playing. No stockings were hung. Several days before Christmas, Dad took my brother and me to the large department store in town and told us to pick out something for Christmas. That was all he could do that year.

Although much sadness, loneliness, and loss surrounded that year's Christmas, it remains as one of the most profound Christmas seasons in my life. It was that year that I came to understand what the name Immanuel really meant—God with us. Every time I remember that Christmas, I am moved by the truth that has been treasured in my heart. Of all the names Jesus is called, none may be clearer than Immanuel: God with us.

Not God near us. Not God aware of us. Not God close by. But God *with* us.

In every situation. In every moment. In every season. Always.

As I ponder that story from many years ago, the treasure I find is the truth of God's presence in my life. So take a few minutes together and talk about this question as it invites you to remember. And as you remember, see what treasures have been locked away in your hearts. Some of those treasures will lead you to see the place of Immanuel—where God was, and still is, with you.

Merry Christmas!

Christmas waves a magic wand over this world, and behold, everything is softer and more beautiful.

—Norman Vincent Peale, as quoted in
A Chicken Soup for the Soul Christmas,
by Jack Canfield and Mark Victor Hansen

LOOKING FOR MORE?

Check out www.50Fridays.com and find other resources
to help you intentionally grow an authentic and intimate marriage.

At www.50Fridays.com you will find:
The 50 Fridays Intimacy Challenge
Fun Friday Date Nights
An interactive blog with Jeff and Lora

- - - - -

Pastors and Church Leaders

At www.50Fridays.com we offer practical ways
to use this book to help grow marriages in your church.

Sermon series on marriage
Small group material ideas and curriculum
Retreats and conferences with Jeff and Lora

- - - - -

Speaking

For more information on having Jeff and Lora
speak to your church or organization,
send inquiries to Speaking@50Fridays.com